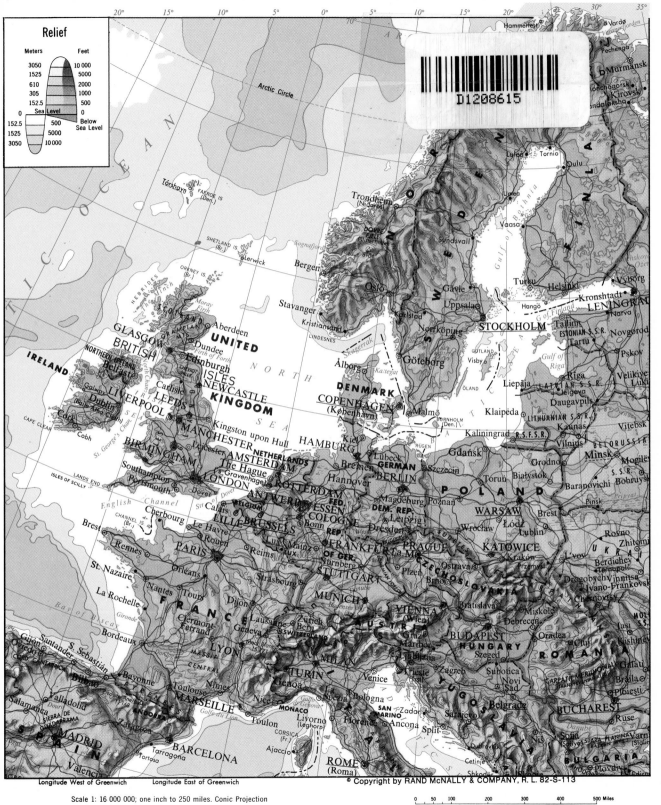

Relief

Meters		Feet
3050		10 000
1525		5000
610		2000
305		1000
152.5		500
0	Sea Level	0
152.5		500	Below
1525		5000	Sea Level
3050		10 000

Longitude West of Greenwich   Longitude East of Greenwich

© Copyright by RAND McNALLY & COMPANY, R. L. 82-S-113

Scale 1: 16 000 000; one inch to 250 miles. Conic Projection

Elevations and depressions are given in feet

| 0 | 50 | 100 | 200 | 300 | 400 | 500 Miles |

| 0 | 100 | 200 | 400 | 600 | 800 Kilometers |

Enchantment of the World

ENGLAND

By Carol Greene

Consultant: C. Aidan MacDermot, former Information Officer for the British Consulate-General in Chicago and executive with the British Broadcasting Corporation in London

Consultant for Social Studies: Donald W. Nylin, Ph.D., Assistant Superintendent for Instruction, Aurora West Public Schools, Aurora, Illinois

Consultant for Reading: Robert L. Hillerich, Ph.D., Bowling Green State University, Bowling Green, Ohio

Chapter titles in this book are from King Richard II *(Act 2, Scene 1), a play by William Shakespeare, who was one of England's—and the world's—greatest poets.*

 CHILDRENS PRESS, CHICAGO

In London you can see the pearly queen (left) in the east end or eat your lunch in the park (opposite).

For Charles Rehkopf

Library of Congress Cataloging in Publication Data

Greene, Carol.
England.

(Enchantment of the world)
Includes index.
Summary: Describes some of England's most
charming features in the areas of geography,
history, scenic treasures, culture, industry,
and people.
1. England—Description and travel—
1971- —Juvenile literature. 2. Great
Britain—History—Juvenile literature.
[1. England] I. Title. II. Series.
DA632.G74   942   82-4471
ISBN 0-516-02763-8   AACR2

Picture Acknowledgments
Colour Library International: Cover, pages 4, 5, 6, 8, 9, 10,
11, 12, 14, 15, 19, 21, 22, 24, 25, 27, 28, 30, 33 (2 photos), **38,**
39 (2 photos), 43, 44, 46, 48 (2 photos), 49, 50, 51 (2
photos), 54, 55, 56, 59, 63, 64 (2 photos), 65, 66 (3 photos),
67 (3 photos), 69, 71, 73, 74, 76, 78, 79, 80, 81, 82, 85, 86, 87,
88 (2 photos), 90, 91, 94, 97, 100 (2 photos), 103, 104, 105 (2
photos), 108, 109
Wide World Photos: page 60 (2 photos)
Jerome Wyckoff: page 122
**Flag on back cover courtesy Flag Research Center,
Winchester, Massachusetts 01890**
Cover: A view of London showing the Houses of
Parliament and the river Thames

TABLE OF CONTENTS

The countryside in Cumbria County

Chapter 1

THIS ENGLAND

ISLAND IN THE MIST

You look out the plane window, eager for a first glimpse. And you see—nothing. Nothing but thick gray fog. You sit back, disappointed. Is *this* what England is like? But a moment later you bounce back up. Sun glints off the plane wing. You look down and see—England.

It's a crazy quilt—patches of green and gold and brown sewed together any which way. The fields are all shapes and sizes. What are the dark green lines separating them? Hedges! Many farmers in England still use hedgerows instead of fences. And what about the barely-visible tiny white polka dots? Why they must be sheep!

Now far below is a town. But surely it isn't real. It looks like a toy village with thatch-roofed cottages, crooked streets, and—a *castle!* Maybe it's a village built for tourists, the kind that shows how people used to live. But, no. There's another village. It looks just as unreal.

Here's the fog again. You sit back, and can't wait to land. You aren't visiting some make-believe place built just for tourists. This is *England*—and it is real.

The Bank of England is in the left foreground.

ISLAND OF OLD AND NEW

What to do first? Start by visiting the Old Lady of Threadneedle Street in London. She won't mend your coat or patch your jeans, though. She's there to take care of money. The Old Lady of Threadneedle Street is another name for the Bank of England.

Then take a boat trip along the river Thames. (Be sure to call it the *Tehmz*.) Stop off at Hampton Court. This palace was given to King Henry VIII by a man who thought Henry was after his head. You have to cross a bridge to get over the moat. Look at the creatures lining the bridge—lions, griffins, and other fabulous beasts. They're known as "the king's beasts." There are supposed to be ghosts in the palace, too. Henry had a nasty habit of killing some of his wives. (He had six of them, one at a time.) Maybe some of them *did* come back to haunt his royal home.

Hampton Court's formal garden

Wander out to the gardens. Another crazy quilt! Bed after bed of flowers of every color spread out down to the river's edge. There's a bush shaped like a fat little mushroom. And a group of bushes that look like upside-down tops.

A boat is leaving. Next stop, Runnymede. *That's* an important place, history books say. It's where a group of noblemen forced King John to sign the Magna Carta in 1215. That document gave the English rights that everybody ought to have.

Oxford Street is one of the busiest shopping areas in London.

THE MISTS OF HISTORY

One can't get to many places in England without bumping into history. It's everywhere. English people even drive on the left side of the road because of history. Centuries ago, when they still rode horses and carried swords, travel wasn't always safe. A man preferred to have his sword arm between him and whoever might be coming from the opposite direction. So, since most people were right-handed, they rode on the left side of the road. And they just haven't bothered to change.

For some really ancient history, travel to Salisbury Plain in southern England. Here in a circle stand huge blocks of stone. Each weighs 40 to 50 tons (36 to 45 metric tonnes). They came from Marlborough Downs, 24 miles (39 kilometers) away. They were dragged here by men four thousand years ago. Those men didn't have horses or carts or even wheels. Inside the circle are bluish stones. They weigh about 5 tons (4.5 metric tonnes) each. These stones came from Wales. They had to be brought 250 miles (402 kilometers) over both land and water.

A lot of mysteries—and a lot of history—still surround Stonehenge.

The name of this strange monument is Stonehenge. It means "the hanging stones." For centuries people have wondered why it was built in the first place. An astronomer named Gerald Hawkins figured out one answer with a computer. He showed that when the stones are lined up with the sun and the moon, they make a sort of calendar. It can be used to tell when the different seasons will begin. It even tells when eclipses will occur. Not everyone agrees with Hawkins, though.

For more ancient history, visit Torquay farther west. Fossils of cave bears, mammoths, and woolly rhinoceroses have been found here. Or go to Cheddar Gorge and see the twelve-thousand-year-old skeleton of a man. (You also could eat some genuine cheddar cheese there.)

ISLAND OF SEAS AND FLOWERS

Go on to Cornwall. Smugglers once lived here. Looking at the rocky shore and angry waves, it's easy to believe they must have been brave to make a living that way. But bravery isn't unusual for folk in Cornwall. For centuries they've taken care of themselves on the sea. Often they've taken care of other people, too.

It's not easy for boats to make their way through rough water like this. Many have been wrecked on the rocks. The Cornish people posted watchers during storms. When the watchers saw a boat in trouble, they'd rush out to it in lifeboats. They would save as many survivors as they could. Even in a storm today the Cornish wait uneasily for fireworks. That's the signal for another wreck. Everyone who can runs down to the water to carry out another rescue mission.

At low tide on a quiet day, walk across a causeway off the Cornwall coast. Climb St. Michael's Mount. Here is a castle that looks as if it came straight out of a fairy tale.

Thirty miles (forty-five kilometers) off the Cornish coast lie the Isles of Scilly. There are 150 of them, but people live on only five. The largest of the populated islands is St. Mary's. Waves foam against its sandy beaches, while inland the fields foam with daffodils, iris, and narcissus. These fields are flower farms. Their sweet-smelling crops are shipped to other parts of England still held in the grip of cold weather.

For more gardens full of early spring flowers, travel to Kent. It's in the southeastern part of England. Other crops are grown here, too. In a way, Kent is like one big garden for the city of London to the north.

St. Just, Cape Cornwall in Cornwall County

Devon, in southwestern England, has a moist climate and is usually warm throughout the year.

Before going to Kent, though, you really should visit Devon. It is right next to Cornwall. Devon is the home of some truly fierce English mists, especially on the moors. (A moor is a large area of open grassland.) It was on Devon's Dartmoor that Sir Arthur Conan Doyle set his spooky Sherlock Holmes's tale, *The Hound of the Baskervilles.*

Take a twelve-mile (nineteen-kilometer) boat trip from Devon's coast to the island of Lundy. True, Lundy used to swarm with pirates, but they're gone now. Instead, watch the swarms of sea birds on the rocks.

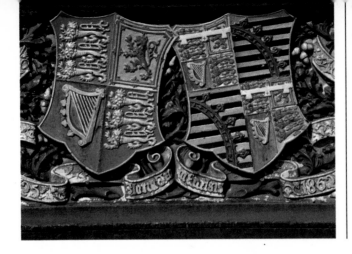

Coats of arms

ISLAND OF WOOD AND STONE

England's cities and towns are as full of stories and interesting sights as is her countryside. In Bath Abbey in the town of Bath, ladders run up the church's buttresses. The builder put them there for angels to climb. In St. Mary Redcliffe, a church in Bristol, there's a monument to the church cat.

In Coventry is a statue of Lady Godiva, a noblewoman who rode naked through the streets in the eleventh century. She wanted to convince her husband, a local ruler, that he should be kinder to his people. Legend says that everyone was impressed by her bravery. So no one looked at her—except for one man. He became known as Peeping Tom and he immediately went blind.

Other stories are told in city streets by puppets such as Punch and Judy. These characters have been traveling around for hundreds of years on the hands of puppeteers. They love to make children—and grown-ups—laugh.

Stories also are told on coats of arms. They hang in many places in England. Back in the days when knights wore armor, it was hard to tell a friend from an enemy on the battlefield. So men began wearing cloth tunics over their armor. On these tunics were emblems that told which family a knight belonged to. A knight from the Wood family might have a tree as his emblem. A knight

15

from the Armstrong family might have three strong arms as his. After a while, more detailed coats of arms were designed. To begin with, though, they simply served a useful purpose.

ISLAND OF HEROES

Everywhere in England there are statues and pictures and plaques. They honor heroes from the past. England has produced some very great heroes. But not all of them have been soldiers or statesmen or artists or scientists. Some have been quite ordinary people who did brave things just because they felt they had to be done. Thousands of English people were heroes of that sort during World War I and World War II. Back in 1665 and 1666 there were heroes like that in the little Midlands village of Eyam.

In those days the dreadful bubonic plague was sweeping through England. No one knew a cure for it then. People who caught it died a horribly painful death. For a time the 350 inhabitants of Eyam were safe. The plague hadn't reached the Midlands or northern England. Then one day the village tailor opened some cloth from London. It was infected. Soon the tailor came down with the terrible disease.

"What shall we do?" the villagers asked one another. "We have to get away! Let's go to some other village. We'll be safe there."

"No," said the rector of the village church. "We can't go anyplace else. We might carry the plague with us."

He was right and the villagers knew it. So they swallowed their fear and stayed in Eyam. By the time the plague had passed, three fourths of them had died, including the rector's wife. But the rest of the Midlands and northern England were safe. The plague did not spread there, thanks to the heroes of Eyam.

Chapter 2

THIS FORTRESS BUILT BY NATURE

A LITTLE WORLD

England is one part of the United Kingdom of Great Britain and Northern Ireland. The other parts are Wales, Scotland, and Northern Ireland. (The rest of Ireland is an independent republic. It rules itself.) The United Kingdom of Great Britain and Northern Ireland lies on islands across the English Channel from France.

England is separated from Scotland by the river Tweed, the Cheviot Hills, and the Solway Firth. (A firth is a narrow arm of the sea.) It is separated from Wales by a man-made border. And it is separated from Ireland by the Irish Sea.

England—once you take a good look—is one of the most interesting countries in the world. It's hard to believe that a country so packed with history, heroes, booming cities, and beautiful scenery is about the same size as Greece or the state of Alabama. England has only 50,362 square miles (130,438 square kilometers) of land. That's small, as countries go.

England's smallness is one of the most important facts about her. Because there isn't much land, the English have had to be very careful about using what there is. Through the centuries they have worked hard to develop new and better farming methods. Even so, they must import much of what they need to feed themselves and to use as raw materials in industry.

Trade became important early in English history. The seas were the roads that led to sources of trade. The English always have been at home on the sea. For several centuries they could boast that they had the best navy in the world.

The need for foreign trade also caused the English to send out explorers such as Sir Francis Drake and Sir Walter Raleigh. Eventually England ruled a vast group of nations known as the British Empire. "The sun never sets on the British Empire" was a saying. It was true, because at one time England had colonies in every part of the world.

Because of her size, England also has had to be clever about using natural resources. In the sixteenth century wood for fuel started running low. By the seventeenth century England had turned to coal, and mining became an important industry. Now, in addition to coal and oil, nuclear reactors are used as sources of energy in England.

GIFTS FROM THE SEA

The second really important fact about England is that it is part of an island. Before the days of airplanes, the only way European enemies could attack England was by sea. It's a lot easier to pick off enemies when they're sitting in boats, in plain sight, than when they're sneaking through hills and forests. That's why Shakespeare called England "this fortress built by Nature."

The Lizard, the southernmost point in England, has a rugged coastline.

Being part of an island has been important to England in other ways, too. If you look at a map of the world, you'll see that England lies quite far to the north. It is as far north as Edmonton, Alberta, in Canada and Novosibirsk in Siberia. That should make England a bitterly cold place.

But it isn't. Its climate is warmed by the Gulf Stream—now known as the North Atlantic Drift. This warm ocean current begins in the Caribbean Sea and flows through the Gulf of Mexico and the Straits of Florida. Then it travels northward along the east coast of the United States to Cape Hatteras, North Carolina. From there, it is pushed by southwesterly winds all the way across the Atlantic Ocean. When the current reaches the British Isles, it almost surrounds them and it warms the cooler air above.

So in winter, temperatures in England average about 40 degrees Fahrenheit (4.4 degrees Celsius). In summer they average about 60 degrees Fahrenheit (15.6 degrees Celsius). This creates a long growing season, which is important for agriculture.

"Well, it sure felt a lot colder than that," visitors might grumble—and they'd be right. That's also because England is an island. Besides bringing much warmer temperatures, the sea also brings much dampness. Damp cold can feel a lot colder than dry cold.

English people are used to their climate, though. They tend to get a little panicky if temperatures climb as high as the 70s (low 20s Celsius) in the summer. In winter they like to warm their houses to about 62 degrees Fahrenheit (16.7 degrees Celsius) which feels downright chilly to visitors from Rome or Atlanta.

English people are used to fast changes in their weather, too. A drizzly day can suddenly turn sunny, then go back to being drizzly again. They're used to the fogs, although the Clean Air Act

The Houses of Parliament, on the banks of the river Thames, loom through the fog.

of 1956 has reduced the amount of smoke in the air. It has made fogs less dangerous to people's health.

The English are used to seasons that change slowly. Spring flowers can bloom for months in England. But most of all, the English are used to a climate that keeps their island a brilliant green most of the time. It allows them to grow things for ten months out of the year.

Of course the sea brings England other gifts, too. The fishing industry plays a big role in determining what English people eat. And vacations by the sea aren't at all unusual for the English. After all, no place in England is very far from the sea!

THE FACE OF ENGLAND

If you look at a map of Great Britain and cover up Scotland and Wales, the tall bumpy triangle that's left is England. Running down the middle from the border with Scotland to about the center of England is a range of mountains called the Pennine Chain. They're sometimes known as "the backbone of England."

The top of the triangle, northern England, is a place of wild beautiful scenery and busy areas of industry. One of the jewels of northern England is the Lake District. Here rugged mountains and quiet lakes surround the home of England's great poet William Wordsworth.

In the center of England lies a large area called the Midlands. Four rivers surround the Midlands: the Thames on the south, the Trent on the north, the Severn on the west, and the Ouse on the east. The ground here rolls in gentle hills and valleys. The farmers have good soil and growing conditions.

No place in England is very far from the sea.

The big bulge on the map east of the Midlands is East Anglia. It is a flat, marshy country. It might remind you of its neighbor, Holland, across the North Sea. Canals crisscross East Anglia and you may even see a windmill.

At the bottom of the bulge, the river Thames flows into the sea. Fifty miles (eighty kilometers) inland on the banks of the Thames sits the great port city of London.

South of London lies warmer country. To the east the land is broken by lines of low hills called scarplands and hilly grasslands called downs. The coast of southern England borders the English Channel. Here the hills drop off into cliffs of limestone and chalk, including the famous White Cliffs of Dover.

The western part of southern England is rugged. It is one of the warmest places in the country because it is so close to the North Atlantic Drift. Along its coasts are many seaside resorts.

Visitors can see the White Cliffs of Dover when they arrive in England by boat.

Several small islands also are part of England. The most important are the Isles of Scilly off the coast of Cornwall in the southwest and the Isle of Wight off the southern coast.

Gardening is more than just a hobby with the English. It's a passion. England practically bursts with flowers, from purple seas of heather on the moors to pools of bluebells and white clouds of black thorn blossoms in the countryside. Even in the cities there are carefully tended rose gardens and window boxes dripping with petunias and geraniums. Marshy East Anglia manages to raise more tulips than Holland does.

A few of England's stately homes have especially beautiful gardens. All of these mansions used to belong to private families. Now many of them are owned and kept up by the National Trust, a government agency founded to preserve England's heritage. Some stately home gardens contain mazes made of tall hedges (where lovers are supposed to meet).

The English are proud of their countryside. They take the Litter Act of 1958 very seriously. Another act bans billboards in most areas. There are 2.5 million acres (1,011,715 hectares) of forest and woodland in England. You can find oak, beech, chestnut, elm, lime, cedars of Lebanon, and even a few palm trees.

BURIED TREASURE

As beautiful as England is, some of its most important treasures are underground. Along the Pennine Chain of mountains lie large coal fields. Beneath the East Midlands and the northern county of Cumberland is iron ore. Both oil and gas have been found beneath the North Sea. Clay for pottery and chalk and limestone for cement help the economy in the southwestern part of the country.

The English people love all kinds of animals. A young man feeds the pigeons in Trafalgar Square in London.

ALL CREATURES GREAT AND SMALL

Of course, England has the usual domesticated animals, all those that James Herriot writes about in his books, such as *All Creatures Great and Small.* English people are extremely fond of animals, especially dogs, cats, and horses. They also make pets of hamsters and mice, goldfish and turtles, and birds. One unusual animal the English sometimes tame as a pet is the hedgehog. It's a small animal, about 10 inches (254 millimeters) long. It is covered with quills.

The English love to bird-watch. With 230 different kinds of resident birds, plus 200 kinds of migrants who drop in for part of the year, they have a lot to watch. Most popular is the robin, a much smaller bird than its American cousin. Poems have been written about the nightingale, which sings its lovely song after dark. Other poems honor the skylark, which greets the dawn. In the evening the blackbird and the thrush announce the coming of night. Come spring, people keep a sharp eye out for the cuckoo, a migrant that announces summer is near. Sparrows chitter along city streets in England; pigeons gather in Trafalgar Square in London; and gulls soar in from the sea.

The English have their share of insects—more than twenty thousand kinds. But they have only three species of snakes. Only one snake, the adder, is poisonous. Fortunately, it's also rather rare.

Chapter 3

THIS ROYAL THRONE
OF KINGS

WAVE OF TRIBES

No one knows exactly where they came from or when they came—those people in England more than ten thousands years ago. Of course, England wasn't called England then. It had no name at all. It was joined to the rest of Europe by a long marshy arm of land. That's probably how the first settlers got there. But one day the sea flooded the arm of land and an island was born.

The people on the island lived in caves, in spaces between rocks, and in pits dug into the ground, circled with stones and covered with branches and sod. They were hunters who went after their prey with rough stone axes and sharp sticks. The animals they killed were used for food to eat and skins to wear.

Then between 8000 and 3000 B.C., people from Spain and the part of France called Brittany set sail in little skin-covered boats for the shores of England. They settled on hilltops in the southern and western parts. These people knew how to weave and make pottery. More important, they knew how to plant grain and make it into flour. They didn't only hunt animals. They raised and cared for cattle and sheep. Their homes were round huts. Near these huts they erected huge stone monuments, called dolmens, to honor the spirits they worshiped.

In the 1970s this group of people lived as the ancient Britons did in the third century B.C. They produced their own food and learned pottery making, weaving, and metal work. Behind them is their communal hall.

About 2000 B.C., a new wave of people made their way to England. They came from the Rhine and Danube river areas in eastern Europe. They are known as the Beaker Folk because of drinking vessels (beakers) archaeologists have found buried with their dead. The Beaker Folk knew about metal and made bows, arrows, and bronze weapons. At first they used these weapons to fight the hilltop people. Later the two groups made peace and began marrying one another. It may have been the Beaker Folk who built the strange, towering circle of stones called Stonehenge.

For several hundred years the island people lived solitary lives. They were cut off and safe from the rest of the world. Then around 700 B.C., the fierce Celts began crossing the English Channel. The Celts were divided into a number of tribes. The first tribe to arrive was the Gaels. They moved into the northern and western parts. Then came the Brythons. They took over the south and east. They drove the Beaker Folk into the hills and forests in the west.

The Celts knew how to make swords, shields, and chariots. They used them often, for no sooner had they conquered the Beaker Folk than they started fighting one another.

But the Celts didn't spend all their time fighting. They also made plows (pulled by oxen), farmed, and raised bees. They mined tin and other metals. They traded with merchants who sailed from the lands around the Mediterranean Sea. For money they used iron bars. The Celts had their own religion, too, based on the worship of nature gods. They called their priests "druids." One of their ancient rituals, Samain, is the origin of Halloween.

The Celts were light-skinned, fair-haired people. They loved to dress up in bright woolen clothes. They made beautiful jewelry, shaped of metal, painted with enamel, and studded with precious stones. Both men and women wore their hair in long braids. The men were very proud of their huge mustaches. For battle the men painted their bodies with a blue dye called woad.

ROME TAKES CHARGE

In 55 B.C., the proud Roman general Julius Caesar decided to invade the island he called Britannia. He'd heard about the riches to be found there and wanted to take some back to Rome. Besides, the island people had been helping their friends across the English Channel, the Gauls, fight against Rome. So Caesar sailed his Roman legions, including cavalry, across the channel to attack the blue-painted Celts. The invasion was doomed from the start. His legions became seasick. Finally Caesar gave up and went back to Gaul. He tried another invasion in 54 B.C., but again he lost.

Not until ninety-seven years later, in A.D. 43, did the Roman emperor Claudius manage to conquer the island people and set up colonies.

This time the Romans meant to stay—and they did. They built cities and towns, fortresses and roads. Some of the roads are still in use. They put up public baths, theaters, temples, and beautiful villas. They erected walls to protect their colonies from other invaders. One of these, Hadrian's Wall, ran across the north of Britannia. It kept out the Picts, who lived in Scotland. Sections of this wall still exist along the border with Scotland.

Eventually the island people accepted their Roman conquerors. Christianity came to Britannia and for four hundred years the people prospered. Then the Romans began to hear of barbarian invasions back home. Early in the fifth century they had to leave Britannia. Soon the island found itself in deep trouble.

A Roman ruin (above) has been uncovered in London. Hadrian's Wall (below) ran across the north of Britannia to keep out invaders.

DANGER FROM THE SEA

Once again invaders poured into Britain—Picts from Scotland,
Scots who had come from Ireland, and, worst of all, Angles,
Saxons, and Jutes from Germanic countries. These last three tribes
chose the southern and eastern parts of Britannia for their
settlements. The Brythons (now called Britons) fought hard for a
hundred years. Under the leadership of such chiefs as Arthur,
they thought they could win. But the new invaders kept pushing.
At last the Britons were forced into the northern and western
parts of the country. Arthur became part of a glorious legend and
the island had a new name—Angle-land, or England.

Eventually the Angles and Saxons formed into seven tribal
nations, each with its own king. The nations were East Anglia,
Essex, Kent, Mercia, Northumbria, Sussex, and Wessex. Usually
one of them controlled the other six. King Egbert of Wessex, the
last tribal king is often called the first king of England.

About 800, invaders struck again, this time from Denmark.
They trampled all of England except Wessex, which was ruled by
a powerful king called Alfred the Great. In 886 Alfred defeated the
Danes. He drove them into the northeastern part of England,
which was then named the Danelaw. After Alfred's death,
though, the Danes gained power again. Canute, brother of the
king of Denmark, took the throne until 1035. In 1042 Edward the
Confessor, a Saxon, became king. He ruled until his death in 1066.

THE NORMANS

Again England was in trouble. Edward had no children, so the
English noblemen chose a man called Harold to be their king. But

William, duke of Normandy in France, said Edward had promised the throne to him. When the English ignored him, William invaded. Leading an army of Normans, he defeated Harold at the Battle of Hastings. On Christmas Day, 1066, he became king and from then on was known as William the Conqueror.

William was grateful to the Normans who helped make him king. He gave them important jobs. He also gave them most of the land. The defeated Anglo-Saxons were forced to work as serfs. William built many cathedrals and castles. He conducted a huge survey (set down in the *Domesday Book*) to find out how much property he had and how much money he could demand as taxes.

When William died in 1087, his son William II became king. After that, William II's brother Henry I ruled. A man called Stephen was crowned in 1135 and then civil war broke out. The nobles were tired of having a king tell them what to do. Each wanted to rule over his own property and its people. And they almost won.

THE GREAT CHARTER

In 1154, a man from the Plantagenet family became King Henry II. He won back power from the nobles. But he went too far when he made plans to rule the Catholic Church, too. Some of his men killed Thomas à Becket, the Archbishop of Canterbury, while Becket was praying in the cathedral. This made the people so angry that Henry had to grant many special favors to the church.

From 1189 to 1199, Richard I (called Richard the Lionhearted) was king. But he spent most of his time in the Holy Land, fighting in the Third Crusade to make Christians of the people there. Meanwhile, his brother John ruled in England. Nobody liked

John, who was a cruel man. When he became king, a group of
nobles opposed him and won. At Runnymede they forced him to
sign the Magna Carta (Great Charter). The charter lists certain
rights that are granted to the people.

The people won another victory when Edward I became king in
the late 1200s. He set up the Model Parliament. This was a group
of nobles, churchmen of all ranks, knights, and townspeople who
met to discuss the country's problems. They had the power to veto
taxes the king wanted to levy.

Edward also managed to conquer Wales, although he failed to
do the same with Scotland. He increased England's prestige at
home and abroad by granting royal charters to the universities at
Oxford and Cambridge.

WAR FOR A HUNDRED YEARS—AND THEN SOME

In 1337, England and France began to battle each other; they
didn't stop until 1453. It started when Edward III decided he
wanted the French throne, too, because his mother's brothers
were French kings. Richard II continued the war when he became
king. Meanwhile, the English people were paying extremely high
taxes. In 1381, a workingman called Wat Tyler led a revolution of
popular protest. He failed, but soon afterward Richard had to give
up his throne and Henry IV became king. Henry ignored the war
with France as much as possible. But his son, Henry V, threw
himself into it. He went so far as to rule France as regent for a
time. After he died, the French decided they'd had enough of
English rulers. Eventually a young French girl called Joan of Arc
led her country in the first of many victories against England.

War with France was over, but back home a new war was just

36

beginning. Henry VI, a member of the Lancaster family, had become king in 1422. But he was a weak ruler and the York family decided it could provide a better king. This war lasted from 1455 till 1485, with the crown bouncing from one family to the other. It was called the War of the Roses because the Lancaster family emblem was a red rose and the York family emblem a white rose. The argument finally was settled in 1485 when Henry, a member of the Tudor family, killed Richard III of York in battle and became Henry VII.

THE BIRTH OF A CHURCH

Henry VII kept his people happy. He also established good relations with other countries—mostly by marrying his children to members of foreign royal families. By the time his son, Henry VIII, became king, the English royal family was rich. Henry VIII let Thomas Cardinal Wolsey, the Roman Catholic Archbishop of York, run the country. At times it seemed the king was more interested in the arts, eating, drinking, and hunting.

Then Henry decided to divorce his wife, Catherine of Aragon, and marry Anne Boleyn. The pope, head of the Roman Catholics, refused to grant the divorce. So Henry got rid of Wolsey. (Wolsey is the man who gave Henry the palace at Hampton Court in an effort to save his own head.) Church leaders in England weren't entirely against Henry's idea. An anti-Catholic movement called the Reformation was spreading across Europe and they liked many of its Protestant ideas. So the Church of England was born. But Henry's new marriage didn't last. After less than three years he had Anne Boleyn beheaded on charges of treason. He took four more wives before he died in 1547.

Trade, exploration, and the arts advanced during the reign of Elizabeth I, sometimes called the golden age of English history.

THE GOLDEN AGE

Anne Boleyn left her country an important treasure. Her daughter by Henry VIII, Elizabeth, became one of the greatest monarchs England has ever had. Elizabeth I was crowned queen in 1558. At once she began programs to benefit the people she ruled and loved. Trade flourished and the great East India Company was formed. Explorers such as Sir Francis Drake and Sir Walter Raleigh set sail to reap the riches of the New World. The powerful Spanish navy, the Armada, was defeated when it attacked England. The arts—especially literature—blossomed with the works of such geniuses as William Shakespeare.

Portraits of two British kings, Henry VIII (left) and Charles I (right)

THE ROUNDHEADS AND THE CAVALIERS

After Elizabeth died without heirs in 1603, her cousin James VI, the king of Scotland, became James I, king of England. The English did not like James I. He believed that kings received the right to rule directly from God and not from the people they ruled. His son, Charles I, even refused to let Parliament meet for a number of years. Finally, in 1642, the country erupted in civil war. People on the king's side were called Cavaliers. People who supported Parliament were mostly Puritans. They were called Roundheads because of the way they cut their hair. The Puritans won the war and beheaded Charles. England now was known as the Commonwealth of England. Its ruler, the lord protector, was a man called Oliver Cromwell.

The problem with Cromwell and the other Roundheads was that they tried to force their religious beliefs on everyone else. By the time Cromwell died in 1658 and his son Richard took over, the English wanted someone on the throne again. A general called George Monk overthrew the government, and in 1660 Charles II (son of Charles I) became king.

Chapter 4

THIS SCEPTER'D ISLE

A UNITED KINGDOM

Dreadful things happened during the reign of Charles II. There was the Great Plague of 1665 and the Great Fire of London in 1666. But good things happened, too, especially in the areas of justice and government. The Habeas Corpus Act was passed in 1679. It stated that arrested persons could not be kept in prison for a long time before being brought before a court. Parliament also began to gain more and more power.

When Charles II died in 1685, his brother James became king. James II was a Roman Catholic. He wanted everybody else in England to be one, too. Parliament disagreed and invited James's Protestant daughter, Mary, and her husband, William of Orange, ruler of The Netherlands, to share the English throne. James II fled to France. From that day on, Parliament had the right to approve or disapprove the monarchs who would rule England. Since this change came about without any bloodshed, it was known as the Glorious Revolution of 1688.

Soon after William died, his sister-in-law Anne became queen. England banded together with other European countries to fight Spain and France. New colonies in Canada and the Mediterranean soon came under English rule. The hero of this war was the duke of Marlborough. Meanwhile, another important event changed English maps. In 1707 the Act of Union was passed. It declared that England, Scotland, and Wales were all one kingdom. It was called the United Kingdom of Great Britain.

GROWING PAINS

While Anne still was queen, an act was passed that said no Roman Catholic could be ruler of England. When Anne died in 1714, her nearest Protestant relative received the crown. He was George I, a German prince who unfortunately couldn't speak English. So he chose a council of ministers. The chief minister, Sir Robert Walpole, governed the country. This was the beginning of the British cabinet system of government. Walpole is known as the first prime minister.

George I's son, George II, didn't want to be in charge either, but *his* son, George III, wanted to regain the old powers of the king. When George III came to the throne, England owned territory all over the world. Another war with France had brought her much of India, Canada, and all the French possessions east of the Mississippi River in America.

In 1776 the American colonies rebelled. The Revolutionary War in America dragged on much longer than most people in England thought it should have. They wanted George to pull out England's forces. But he refused and at last he lost the war. With that defeat England lost some of its most valuable possessions.

Two other revolutions were going on in England at the same time. One was the Industrial Revolution, which began in the 1700s in the textile industry. Machines that could produce cloth were invented. Soon fewer and fewer people were working at home. Instead they worked in factories. Around the factories sprang up cities and towns. Factory machines needed fuel for power, so the coal mining industry exploded into activity, too. And both finished goods and raw materials had to be shipped from place to place, so the transportation industry blossomed.

At the same time, the Agricultural Revolution was going on. Many small farms were combined into big ones. Scientific methods of farming were introduced.

While the Industrial Revolution brought England riches, it also brought problems. People in the factory cities lived in filthy slums. Men, women, and children often worked under horrible conditions. (Many of these horrors are described in the novels of Charles Dickens.) Slowly England set itself to solving the workers' problems. A series of Factory Acts improved working conditions. The Mining Act prevented women and children from working in the mines. Acts that made elementary education both required and free also helped the working class.

THE LITTLE EMPEROR

In 1789, the French, inspired by the American revolution, had a revolution of their own. At first the English paid little attention. Then the French revolutionaries became more and more bloodthirsty. They invaded other countries, such as Belgium and The Netherlands. This made Britain nervous. In 1793, England went to war with France.

Soon after, in 1799, a small man who was determined to rule the world became leader of the French. His name was Napoleon Bonaparte.

In 1803, Napoleon decided the time had come to invade Britain.

In Trafalgar Square, London is Nelson's Column, a tall granite column with a stone statue of Horatio Nelson on the top.

But his plans failed. Then in 1805, a tough, one-armed, one-eyed British admiral named Horatio Nelson wiped out Napoleon's entire navy at Trafalgar. Nelson himself was killed in the battle.

Meanwhile, Napoleon was trampling over Austria and Prussia. He set up a treaty with the Tsar of Russia. He hoped to weaken Britain by stopping other nations from trading with her. Britain struck back by blockading France's trade. The United States, France's ally, objected. Britain found herself fighting the U.S. in the War of 1812.

At the same time, Napoleon was marching his Grand Army to Moscow, Russia. He hadn't realized what a powerful enemy the Russian winter would be. Only forty thousand of his half million men made it back to France. At last the duke of Wellington, who had been battling Napoleon in Spain, joined with the Prussians. They crushed the little emperor at the Battle of Waterloo in 1815.

Back in Britain, the English were having trouble with the Irish, who wanted self-rule. That did not fit in with English plans. In 1800, Parliament passed the Act of Union, which abolished the Irish Parliament and set up the United Kingdom of Great Britain and Ireland. Not until 1829, though, were Catholics—and that meant most Irish—allowed to vote or hold office.

Queen Victoria reigned for sixty-three years.

Voting was a big issue in England itself, too. Parliament was controlled by rich landowners. Very few ordinary citizens had the right to vote. The Reform Bill of 1832 changed that. It gave voting rights to most men of the middle class. That meant that five percent of the total population now had something to say about how their country was run.

VICTORIA

Victoria was only eighteen years old when she assumed the British throne in 1837. She reigned for sixty-three years, until 1901. That period of time became known as the Victorian Age. During Queen Victoria's reign free trade was established. The British Empire included about one fourth of all the land in the world and about one fourth of all the people. But there were strict laws controlling trade with British colonies. Sir Robert Peel, who was then prime minister, abolished these laws.

After Peel, two political parties emerged—the Liberal Party and the Conservative Party. With them came two new leaders, William E. Gladstone and Benjamin Disraeli. Victoria had wed her German cousin, Albert. Life at the palace was happy, but unexciting. People found plenty of excitement, though, in the fiery arguments between Gladstone and Disraeli. The two men practically took turns at being prime minister. Under their leadership many reforms were passed and still more lands were added to the British Empire. It was Gladstone who got the vote for most adult males. Disraeli added Cyprus and the Suez Canal to the Empire.

Wars also plagued the Victorian Age. England fought the Crimean War with Russia, a bloody revolution in India, and the Boer War in South Africa.

*David Lloyd George
was prime minister
from 1916 to 1922.*

WORLD WAR I

After Victoria's death, her son Edward VII took the throne. He was known as a pleasure-loving man, but he made a good king. During his reign still more reforms were passed. People felt cheerful and prosperous. Two more political leaders emerged during this time: David Lloyd George, a liberal Welshman, and his younger colleague, Winston Churchill.

Meanwhile in Europe, the Germans felt that the English and French had too much power and riches. So the German Kaiser, Wilhelm II, prepared for war. His plan was to stamp out Belgium and France before anyone could stop him. Into Belgium he marched. The British people were horrified and soon declared war on Germany.

World War I lasted for more than four years. More than twenty allied nations fought against Germany and the Central Powers. Ten million soldiers died, as did a huge number of civilians. New tools of warfare were developed, such as tanks, bomber planes, and the dreaded poison gas. At last, whipped on by the leadership of Lloyd George and strengthened by troops from the United States, England and her allies won. But the price paid was a heavy one, never to be forgotten.

HARD TIMES

During the war everyone had a job to do. But afterwards the jobs disappeared. This was partly because Germany and Russia couldn't afford British goods and partly because the United States and Japan entered the marketplace as strong competitors. At least a million people in England were unemployed for the next seventeen years.

Meanwhile, there was trouble in Ireland, too. The British organized a force called the Black and Tans. (Their clothes were a mixture of khaki uniforms and black police uniforms.) They put down the rebels who wanted an independent Ireland. Lloyd George cooled tempers a bit by signing a treaty that made southern Ireland a dominion. This meant Ireland owed allegiance to the British Crown, but otherwise was free.

The people of northern Ireland did not like this idea. They were mostly Protestant. They didn't want to be part of the new Irish Free State, which was mostly Catholic. So they remained part of the United Kingdom, which changed its name once more, this time to the United Kingdom of Great Britain and Northern Ireland.

Left: King Edward VIII broadcasts his abdication speech.
Above: King George VI and Queen Elizabeth in 1947

In 1936 King George V died. His son became King Edward VIII. But Edward did not keep the throne for long. He wanted to wed a divorced American woman, Mrs. Wallis Warfield Simpson. The government forbade the marriage because of her divorce. Edward gave up the crown and his brother became King George VI.

The whole world watched these romantic happenings with great interest. But other events of a more serious nature were going on in Germany. An Austrian named Adolf Hitler had formed a political group known as the Nazi Party. Soon all of Germany was ringing with his hysterical cries for world rule.

WORLD WAR II

At first no one in England—or in much of the rest of the world—believed it could happen again. Another world war? Impossible! But when Hitler seized Austria, then Czechoslovakia, then Poland, they saw that it *had* happened. In 1939, after the Germans invaded Poland, both Britain and France declared war on Germany. Hitler crushed Norway and The Netherlands in 1940. The British turned to Winston Churchill as their leader.

"I have nothing to offer but blood, toil, tears and sweat," he said.

Winston Churchill was prime minister from 1940 to 1945 and from 1951 to 1955.

Oxford Street after the bombing blitz in April of 1941.

One after another, countries in Europe and North Africa fell to the Germans and Italians, their allies. The Japanese, also allied with Germany, were conquering nations in the Far East. For a long time Britain and her United Kingdom nations held fast. Each night German planes bombed London. Every day the British cleaned up the rubble, buried their dead, and prepared to hold on a little longer. Relief came at last when Hitler made the mistake of invading Russia and the Japanese attacked the United States at Pearl Harbor. Now Britain had powerful allies. By 1945 defeat was turned into victory. Churchill had wanted "victory at all costs." Under him victory was won, but once again the price was high. About 360,000 British people died in the war. Many parts of the country were in ruins, and the economy was seriously weakened.

ENDINGS AND BEGINNINGS

After World War II, Britain could no longer hold on to the Empire. She granted independence to one colony after another.

Poverty at home was a continuing problem. In 1945 the Labour Party introduced social reforms designed to help people from birth to death. By 1951 conditions had improved, only to worsen again in the early 1960s.

England today no longer is the world power she used to be. Some say that England should rid itself of the royal family. But in 1981 when Prince Charles married Lady Diana, people all over the world watched the ceremony on television. Prince Charles is next in line to be king of England.

GOVERNMENT IN ENGLAND

England's government today is a constitutional monarchy. Elizabeth II reigns as queen, but she does not rule. The ruling is done by the cabinet ministers headed by the prime minister. In 1979, a Conservative Party leader, Margaret Thatcher, became the first woman to hold the office of prime minister. Laws in Britain are made by Parliament. The queen merely approves all bills before they become law. Parliament is divided into the House of Commons and the House of Lords. House of Commons members are elected and this house has the most power. Most House of Lords members inherit their seats.

On the local level, the country is divided into administrative counties. These counties are divided into urban and rural districts. Each local unit of government has an elected council that deals with education, roads, and fire and police protection.

The skyline of Liverpool. On the left is the Mersey ferry.

Lake District National Park with Wasdale Fell in the background

Chapter 5

THIS BLESSED PLOT

PERSONALITIES AND PLACES

Throughout history, England has been led by people with strong and colorful personalities. These leaders—the cruel King John, the peace-loving Queen Elizabeth I, the brave and stubborn Winston Churchill—have helped to shape the nation.

Places have personalities, too. They get them partly from the people who live there, but also from the very soil and rocks of which they're made.

TO THE NORTH

There are two sides to the personality of northern England. One is the bustling but sometimes gloomy life of the manufacturing cities and towns. A woman who grew up in the Yorkshire mill town of Elland remembers the color black everywhere. It covered the buildings, people's clothes and faces, the leaves, and even the sheep in the countryside. But she also remembers the golden color of fish and chips, which, she says, were the best in the world.

Antipollution laws and modern manufacturing techniques have cleaned up much of northern England. But manufacturing and the transportation of goods always will be important to such northern cities as Manchester, Liverpool, Leeds, Sheffield, and Newcastle-on-Tyne.

The Pennine Chain, seen in West Yorkshire County,
is called the backbone of England.

The other side of northern England's personality is the wild natural beauty of the Lake District and the Pennine Chain, woodlands with roe deer, badgers, and foxes, and long, silent sweeps of moors.

Some people in northern England hold on to their own special brand of humor. Once a group of farmers in the Yorkshire dales was asked to lend some objects of historical interest to a local exhibition. "Tha can tak me," said one old man.

People who vacation in northern England can go on walking tours around the small lakes and gentle mountains of the Lake District. Or they can rest in secluded inns on the moors. The area is known for its beautiful scenery.

Those who *really* like to walk can tramp 200 miles (322 kilometers) along the Pennine Way, a footpath that leads from the Peak District in the south to the border with Scotland. Less rugged folks can "Meander over the Pennines" (as one ad says) in narrow boats that cruise the Trans-Pennine Canal.

The Royal Pavilion in Brighton

TO THE SOUTH

Southern England also has two sides to its personality. One is the fresh green bloom of growing things—mile after mile of farms and gardens and orchards. The other is the salty tang of the sea. Visitors from Europe who come by boat across the English Channel first see the looming White Cliffs of Dover. Chalk and limestone lie like a deep foundation under this part of England.

In the southeast, the cliffs descend into the rolling hills of the North Downs and the South Downs. (A down is simply a grassy hill.) Tucked away among these hills are many charming little villages.

The southern coast of England is sprinkled with seaside resorts. English people love to spend vacations here. Most popular is Brighton. It's known for its antique shops and its Royal Pavilion.

Stones found in the rocky soil around Dartmoor are used to make fences.

There are a number of port cities along the seacoast. From Southampton the Pilgrims first set sail on the *Mayflower* for the New World. At Portsmouth lies H.M.S. *Victory*, the flagship used by Admiral Lord Nelson at the Battle of Trafalgar.

Southern England, and especially Salisbury Plain, is full of prehistoric remains. It is here that Stonehenge towers in its shroud of mystery. Here too, in Wiltshire, you can see the figure of a huge white horse, cut out of a chalk hill by prehistoric people.

The southwest part of England is made up of more moors, including Dartmoor, Exmoor, and Bodmin Moor, home of wild ponies and picnickers. The main city to the west is Bristol. The weather in this part of England is generally warmer than anywhere else in the country. People flock here to stay in colorful little fishing villages or seaside resorts. Farming is important to the people of southwest England. So is fishing. But many earn their living through the tourist trade.

Going farther west toward Cornwall, you come to Plymouth, on the Devon coast. Cornwall juts into the ocean. The final tip of Cornwall is called Land's End.

TO THE EAST

Visiting East Anglia, that bulge on the map of England north of London, is rather like visiting Holland. Canals, dikes, windmills, tulips, quiet farms—East Anglia has them all. It also has Cambridge, one of the oldest universities in the world.

The coast of East Anglia, which faces the North Sea, is made up mostly of marshes, mud, shingle (stony seashore), and sand dunes. Birds—and bird-watchers—love it.

The weather is fairly dry in East Anglia. But cold winter winds make it one of the chilliest parts of England, especially in the fens (marshes), which often smoke eerily with mist and fog.

IN THE MIDLANDS

The Midlands, which run across the middle of England, make up another area with a personality. It's part heavy, hardworking industry and part farmland. Birmingham is the biggest city in the Midlands and the second biggest city in England. Not far from it is Wolverhampton, another manufacturing center. To the north is the Potteries district, including the city of Stoke-on-Trent. To the northeast are Nottingham and Derby. Manufacturing, obviously, is important to the Midlands. But just as important are cattle, sheep, pigs, and agricultural crops.

One place many people like to visit in the Midlands is Nottingham Castle. The rocky hill, castle walls, and bronze statue of Robin Hood seem to take visitors back through the centuries to the greenwood of merry old England.

The greatest English poet of all, though, lived farther south in a market town on the Avon River, close to the Cotswold Hills. The name of the town is Stratford-on-Avon and the name of the poet is William Shakespeare. Between April and October each year, visitors pack the modern Royal Shakespeare Theatre on the banks of the river to see his timeless plays performed.

THE CATHEDRAL CITIES

All across England towns and cities are nestled around glorious, soaring cathedrals. In the north there's Durham. In the south, there's Winchester (burial place of the Saxon kings), Canterbury,

Canterbury Cathedral is where the archbishop of Canterbury, the spiritual head of the Church of England, has his headquarters.

and Salisbury (with the tallest spire in England). East Anglia boasts a beautiful cathedral at Ely. Each of these cathedrals—and many others—is the origin of fascinating stories. But perhaps the most moving story is that of the cathedral at Coventry.

On a Thursday night, November 14, 1940, German bombers swooped over Coventry and dropped a load of firebombs. The cathedral was hit. By morning only the west tower and outer walls were standing.

"We'll build a new cathedral here when the war is over," said the people of Coventry. On Friday morning they set about cleaning up the rubble. As they worked, they found two pieces of burned roof beam. They put these in the form of a cross. They stuck the cross in a dustbin full of sand for all to see. On the wall behind the cross was carved the words "Father, forgive."

All over the world people heard about "the charred cross of Coventry." To the war-weary people of England it became a sign of hope. The cathedral did not shut down. Sometimes services were held in the burned-out shell, with only the sky for a roof. Meanwhile, money was coming in from everywhere.

In May of 1962 the dream came true. A new, modern cathedral had risen from the ashes of war. Sir Basil Spence, who designed it, did not have it built on the site of the old cathedral. He wanted those ruins to stand as a monument. Services still are held in the ruins on Easter Day. But the new cathedral is also a monument to the belief that some things are stronger than hate. Many, many people worked on it, including fifteen German craftsmen who volunteered their services—free.

LONDON

London—the capital of England and of the United Kingdom of Great Britain and Northern Ireland—is like no place else in the world. It sprawls out like a lazy octopus on the banks of the river Thames, 50 miles (80 kilometers) inland from the sea. Some say it dates back to a Celtic town called Llan Din (which means holy hill). But no one is sure. The Romans called it Londinium and built a wall around it. That part of London is only about 1 square mile (2.6 square kilometers) in area. It is known as The City and is London's center of business. Not many people live in The City, but thousands work there in banks, merchant exchanges, insurance companies, and shipping houses. St. Paul's Cathedral also rises up in The City.

Outside The City, the rest of London also bustles with business and history. In Westminster Abbey, originally built by Edward the Confessor, many English kings and queens have been crowned, married, and buried. Many other famous men and women also have their tombs or monuments in Westminster.

The Tower of London is a great fortress where Queen Elizabeth I and Sir Walter Raleigh were imprisoned and Anne Boleyn was executed. It's not a happy place to visit, but it's awesome. And deep underground, the Crown Jewels are on display.

Not far away is Buckingham Palace. If the Royal Standard is flying, the Queen is in residence there. But even if she isn't, Britons and tourists alike can watch the Changing of the Guard. This is a complicated, impressive ceremony of marching men in red tunics and black bearskin helmets.

Trafalgar Square, famous for its fountains, has a statue of Lord Nelson in the center. English laws are passed in the Houses of

The Houses of Parliament on the river Thames, with Big Ben at the right

Parliament with their famous Clock Tower and bell, Big Ben. In the section of the city called Greenwich, you can set your watch by a clock that determines the right time (called Greenwich mean time) for every other clock in the world.

Important historical items are displayed in the British Museum. In its collection are original manuscripts by almost every famous English writer who ever lived. Less dignified, but more fun, is Madame Tussaud's Wax Museum. This is a collection of lifelike figures of kings, queens, movie stars, murderers, and other people out of history all carved in wax.

For centuries the river Thames was the main road for Londoners. Sight-seeing boats sail along it, past New Scotland Yard, on to Hampton Court and Runnymede, and to Oxford, one of Europe's oldest universities.

Top opposite: *The Tower of London has been a palace, a fortress, and a prison. Today it is a museum and a national monument.*
Bottom opposite: *The Royal Marine Band plays for official functions.*
Above: *Buckingham Palace has been the official home of the royal family since 1837.*

Above: Piccadilly Circus is the center of theater entertainment in London.
Below left: Street markets in London sell all sorts of things, including fresh flowers.
Below right: A busy shopping area in London.

London, the eighth largest city in the world, has antique shops in Hampstead (left), Chinese shops and restaurants in Gerrard Street (below left), and parks, such as St. James's Park (below right).

Chapter 6

THIS PRECIOUS STONE
IN THE SILVER SEA

FROM FIELD TO FACTORY

The very first people to live in England were hunters. Hunting was all they knew how to do and, if they were lucky, it kept them alive. Soon, though, settlers from Spain and Brittany brought with them knowledge of farming, weaving, pottery-making, and animal husbandry. This was the beginning of what is called a "rural economy." For thousands of years most people in England continued to make a living in basic rural occupations.

Of course, a relatively few hardy souls sailed the seas as traders or fished or worked in mines. But most of England's wealth lay in the countryside. And that's where most people lived and worked.

Then, during the 1700s, the age of machines began. A water-powered spinning frame, an iron-smelting furnace that used coke instead of charcoal, and a steam engine were invented. All at once factories sprang up. People rushed from the farms to work in them. The workers needed places to live in, so cities and towns grew up around the factories. The Industrial Revolution was well under way. Life in England never again would be quite the same.

An oil rig in the North Sea

UNDER LAND AND SEA

Mining in England goes back to the Celts. They dug up tin and other metals to trade with foreign merchants. Then in the 1600s, coal became more important as a source of fuel. In 1709, a man called Abraham Darby discovered a way to smelt iron with coke instead of charcoal. This made ironwork more efficient. England became a leader in the iron and steel industry.

English miners still dig for coal, especially along the Pennine Chain. Iron deposits lie in the East Midlands and in the northern county of Cumberland. Although mining still can be a dangerous occupation, strict laws have made it much safer. But neither iron nor coal mining is as important as it once was. High-quality iron ore has almost run out. The steel industry now has to import much of its raw material. Coal is being replaced by new sources of energy, especially natural gas and petroleum.

Natural gas fields lie along the east coast of England. In 1967 the English began to pump gas from wells in the North Sea. Petroleum is another treasure buried under the sea. In 1975 a pipeline began bringing it into the country.

GIFTS OF A NEW AGE

In the far north of England lies the county of Cumberland. There, in a place called Calder Hall, is located a large part of England's dreams for the future. Calder Hall is a nuclear-power station, the first full-scale nuclear-power station in the world. Calder Hall has been supplying England with electricity since 1956. England was the first country in the world to use nuclear power for peaceful purposes. Calder Hall and other stations provide about twelve percent of England's electricity.

Chemistry and physics are other fields in which the English are world leaders. Salt is needed to do chemical work and England has plenty of salt. As a result, chemicals are one of the nation's chief exports. So are isotopes and other radioactive materials.

MADE IN ENGLAND

The English have always been very good at making things. Today, when some of their own natural resources are running out, they import raw materials. They make them into first-rate products and sell them to the people they imported from.

This is especially true when it comes to metal and metal products. Airplanes, automobiles, tractors, engines, machine tools, and scientific instruments flow out of England to countries all over the world.

Shipbuilding on the River Wear in the county of Tyne and Wear

Most factories for the manufacture of these products grew up around the areas where raw materials were found. Cities grew up with them. When many of the raw materials had to be imported, cities such as Birmingham, Wolverhampton, Coventry, Nottingham, and Derby (all in the Midlands) remained great industrial centers. In addition, new factories have been built in other areas, such as London and southern England.

England also is known as a fine builder of ships. Newcastle-

71

on-Tyne in the north is one of the leading cities in this industry. Unfortunately, ships take a lot of steel, and imported iron ore for steel is expensive. As a result, ships have become more expensive and shipbuilding isn't as big a business as it used to be.

The city of Sheffield, also in the north, is one of the great steel-producing centers of England. It is even better-known as a place where fine hand tools, cutlery, scissors, and flatware are made.

The English people make many things to wear—or the cloth to make them with. For several centuries cotton from the United States has entered the busy ports of Liverpool and Manchester (in the northwest). From there the cotton is sent to mills where it is made into cloth. On the other side of the Pennine Chain, wool is the important fiber. For a long time hills and river valleys supplied pastureland for sheep and water power to run mills. Now much of the wool is imported. But cities such as Bradford, Leeds, and Huddersfield continue to make fine woolen cloth.

Some of the most beautiful products made in England come from a district in the Midlands known as the Potteries. Dirty kilns poke up against the sky, tiny houses huddle under coats of soot, and railroad tracks lie in a giant tangle over the ground. It's not a pretty place, but the people who live and work there are cheerful, lively, and very talented. Stoke-on-Trent and the cities and towns around it in the Potteries produce some of the finest china and pottery made anywhere. Expensive stores the world over sell Wedgwood, Spode, and Minton. All come from the Potteries.

THE SILVER SEA

Manufacturing is very important for England's economy. But it wouldn't be if it weren't for trade. Without trade, England

The M1 motorway was the first major expressway built in England.

couldn't get the raw materials she needs. Without trade, she couldn't sell many of the things she makes.

Fortunately, England is in a perfect spot for trading by sea. Southeastern ports like Harwich, Dover, Folkestone, and Southampton are ready and waiting for European ships. Northwestern ports like Liverpool and Manchester welcome ships from the other side of the Atlantic. Manchester, by the way, wasn't always a port. A ship canal that runs from the city to the sea was finished in 1894. Business has been good ever since.

Just as trade is important for manufacturing, transportation is important for trade. Raw materials have to be sent from ports to the places where factories are waiting for them. Then the manufactured goods must be sent back to the ports. England has a web of inland waterways, some of them man-made and some natural. She also has a fine railroad system and good motorways (expressways) for lorries (trucks).

Trade and transportation aren't needed just for manufacturing. Without them the nation would starve. England raises as much food as she can and uses modern scientific methods. But she

Industry and agriculture can be found side by side in England.

simply doesn't have enough farmland to feed all her people. So she imports food, too.

England always has gotten food from the sea. The shallow waters around the coast are good fishing places. Sometimes trawlers go as far as Greenland and Newfoundland. The city of Hull on the Humber Estuary in northern England is one of the main fishing ports. Fleetwood, a town on the Irish Sea, is another.

BACK ON THE FARM

During the Industrial Revolution, the factories drew people away from England's farms. But over the years, factories have produced machines that have improved farming methods. Farms in England are fairly small. The average size is 74 acres (29.9 hectares). But they are worked with the most up-to-date machinery and methods. Soils can be very different, even on the same little farm. That is why many farmers grow several crops instead of a single one.

Animals are important in English agriculture, too. Sheep are raised both for meat and for wool. Cows provide milk and meat. Pigs are another source of meat and chickens provide eggs.

Chapter 7

THIS HAPPY BREED

THE SAME—AND DIFFERENT

People walking along a typical London street don't look very different from people in other large cities.

Occasionally—especially during rush hours—that street becomes crowded. The population of England in the early 1980s was about forty-seven million. About 75 percent of the people live in cities and towns, more than seven million of them in London.

English people are very good at standing in lines. These lines are called "queues" and "to queue" means to stand in line. The English queue at bus stops, in shops, and at theaters. Almost everyone waits patiently, because to push ahead in a queue is considered rude.

Among the crowds on a London street are people of many races and nationalities. There are black people from Africa, brown people from the West Indies, Orientals from Asia, and white people from all over. Since 1950 more than two million immigrants have poured into England. Most are from countries that used to be part of the British Empire. Often they settled in cities, where there simply weren't enough places to live or jobs to go around. In the 1960s, England finally began to limit the number of immigrants that could enter each year.

A policeman, called a bobby, directing traffic in London.

People move around in London in the same ways they do in other parts of the world. They take buses and taxis, ride bikes, and drive cars. (Remember, though, that the English drive their cars on the left side of the road.) The subway system in London, called the underground, is excellent. It is so easy to understand that even a tourist can ride it all alone and not get lost. People leaving London for other parts of England often travel by train. Trains are a very important means of transportation in England.

The names of places in England don't sound like places anywhere else in the world. Where else could one visit towns with names like Chipping Campden, Middleton Stoney, Moreton-in-the-Marsh, Great Badminton, Ditchling, Sharpethorne, Haltwhistle, Chittlehamholt, and Mousehole (pronounced "Mouzle")? Then there's Middle Wallop, Nether Wallop, and Over Wallop. In Bourton-on-the-Water, travelers stay at the Old New Inn.

In England, names often aren't pronounced the way they look. Mr. Featherstonehaugh pronounces his name "Fanshaw." Mrs. Cholmoundley calls herself "Chumly." And the residents of Gloucester say they live in "Glosster."

INFANT SCHOOL TO UNIVERSITY

Children in England must go to school from the age of five till the age of sixteen. Important research in preschool education has taken place in England.

Education in England is supervised by the Department of Education and Science and by local authorities. Ninety percent of English children go to schools that are completely or partly supported by public funds. The other ten percent go to private schools.

Two of England's most famous universities are Oxford (left) and Cambridge (opposite).

Elementary-school-aged children go to primary schools. Everyone used to take a terribly difficult test at the age of eleven. It was called the "eleven-plus exam." Its results determined if a child went on to "grammar school," which was like a high school that prepared students for college; to "secondary-modern school," which taught the usual high-school subjects without aiming toward college admission; or to "technical school," which taught general subjects and gave vocational training, too. Most local education authorities don't require this test anymore. More and more "comprehensive schools" are being built. In these, students who want to prepare for college, students who simply want a good general education, and students who want vocational training all study in the same building.

Universities in England include Oxford and Cambridge, two of the oldest universities in the world, and the University of London, the largest in England, with thirty-six thousand full-time students. There are also technical colleges and special colleges in which students study commerce, the arts, or agriculture.

Left: Spectators crowd stadiums to watch Association football, usually known as soccer.
Opposite: Bowls is played on grass, called a green.

ENGLAND AT PLAY

People in England take sports, and especially team sports, very seriously. Everyone plays on some sort of team at school. People flock by the thousands to watch organized sports on weekends.

One favorite is football. Three million spectators watch their teams battle it out during the season, which runs from August through May. At the end of the season, two teams compete for the Football Association Cup at Wembley Stadium in London. About one hundred thousand folks turn out for that. In addition, there are the international matches with other European teams.

Cricket, though, is the true national sport of England. The game dates all the way back to the 1500s. It is played by two teams with eleven members on each, using a bat and a ball.

Rugby (also called "rugger") is a rather rough sport played by two teams of fifteen members each. The game includes tackling. Since the players wear no pads, they often emerge with a good crop of bruises.

Bowls, or lawn bowling, is not like the game played in a bowling alley. It is played on grass, called a green. The first bowler (player) rolls a jack, or target ball. The other bowlers try to get their bowls as close to the jack as possible. There are hundreds of lawn-bowling clubs in England. Recently indoor games have begun to appear on the scene.

Other favorite sports include field hockey, lacrosse (Canada's national game, invented by North American Indians), swimming, sailing, rowing, tennis, horse racing (with lots of betting, which is legal in England), golf, polo, hiking, horseback riding and jumping, hunting (including fox hunting), and fishing.

Many churches have a cemetery, called a churchyard, next to them.

KIPPERS ANYONE?

Food in England has a bad reputation for being over cooked and tasteless. This isn't quite fair. It's true that some of the cheaper hotels still serve boiled celery to unsuspecting tourists. But you can always nip down the street to the local fish-and-chip shop. The fish is fried and the potatoes are french-fried. They're often served together with vinegar poured over them and rolled up in a cone of newspaper. They're delicious!

Then again, you might try shepherd's pie (a casserole of mashed potatoes and ground meat) or steak and kidney pie (a stew with a pastry crust). Maybe you'll have roast chicken, bangers and mash (thick sausages with mashed potatoes), or fish of some sort (including kippers, which are smoked herring).

SPIRES IN THE CLOUDS

Almost no spot in England is far from a towering cathedral or a quaint little church. Often there is a churchyard (cemetery) next to it.

The Church of England, or Anglican Church, is the official state church. By law the king or queen must belong to the Church of England, but everyone else is free to choose. About twenty-seven million people are baptized members. The spiritual head of the church is the Archbishop of Canterbury. He and the Archbishop of York and twenty-four other bishops are members of the House of Lords. They have something to say about how England is governed. So there isn't a clear separation of church and state.

Other Protestant churches in England are called "Free Churches." The largest are the Baptist, the Congregational, and the Methodist. Sometimes these other Protestant churches are also called "Chapel." A person will say he or she is either "Church" or "Chapel." In other words, he or she belongs either to the Church of England or to another Protestant church. There are also about four million Roman Catholics in England and almost a half million Jews.

PEOPLE RESPONSIBLE FOR PEOPLE

In times gone by, the church and other volunteer organizations began and ran social services, such as schools, hospitals, orphanages, and homes for the elderly. Now, though, all of these and many other programs are taken care of by the government. The National Health Service is funded by taxes. It provides nearly free health care for all. Some people still go to private doctors, but many are happy with the Health Service.

The government also provides a great deal of money for education, subsidized housing, subsidized school meals, care for expectant mothers, and aid to handicapped people. No one is allowed to fall below a certain minimum standard of living. As a result there isn't much poverty. The English people, of course, pay for all of this.

ALBERT HALL AND THE BEATLES

England, as someone has said, is "crawling with culture." The English attend the theater and the ballet, both of which are excellent. They go to concerts in ornate Albert Hall, in the modern Royal Festival Hall, and just about anyplace a concert is given. They go to operas at Covent Garden.

Popular concerts are held in the Royal Albert Hall in London.

Music always has been important to the English. They began with folk songs, many of which still are sung today. In the 1500s and early 1600s, everyone sang madrigals, with "fa-la-la" choruses, bird sounds, and texts about shepherds and shepherdesses. In the late 1600s, Henry Purcell wrote his magnificent church music.

Composers from other countries came to England, too, including George Frederick Handel and J. S. Bach's youngest son (still known as "the English Bach").

In the 1870s William S. Gilbert and Arthur Sullivan began writing operettas that were unlike anything ever written before or since. Their works, such as *The Mikado* and *The Pirates of Penzance*, are loved by people all over the world.

The Beatles in 1966

More recent English composers include such famous people as Benjamin Britten, Frederick Delius, Sir Edward Elgar, Gustav Holst, and Ralph Vaughan Williams.

Then there's the pop scene. It will be a long time before the world forgets four young men from Liverpool on the Mersey River. The Beatles started a whole new thing in pop music. And from England also come The Rolling Stones, The Who, and Pink Floyd — to name just a few.

English people like to go to art galleries, too. Some of their greatest painters are William Hogarth, Thomas Gainsborough, Sir Joshua Reynolds, Joseph Turner, John Constable, Duncan Grant, and Paul Nash.

Lincoln Cathedral has high, pointed arches in the Gothic style of architecture.

Walking tours, bus trips, and expeditions by car or train take the English all over the country. They can see different kinds of architecture in cathedrals, castles, old private homes (many now cared for by the government), and other buildings. Up north might be the remains of a Norman castle with heavy columns and arches like semicircles. Lincoln Cathedral is a good example of the Gothic style, with high pointed arches and spires built to reach up toward heaven.

*Above: The Bell Inn, an Elizabethan building in Suffolk County
Below: St. Paul's Cathedral was completed in 1711. Only one church
is larger than St. Paul's—St. Peter's in Vatican City.*

Elizabethan houses were often "timbered." Wooden frames were filled in with brick and plaster and often formed intricate patterns. Sir Christopher Wren and Inigo Jones were architects of the 1600s who worked in what was called the neoclassical style. St. Paul's Cathedral in London is a good example of this style. Then in the 1700s, the Georgian took over with much brick and stone and simple, balanced designs.

Most Victorian-style buildings (those erected during the time of Queen Victoria) look rather heavy and are full of curlicues and other decorations.

Furniture making used to be an important art in England. Fine pieces still can be seen there today. The most famous furniture makers lived during the 1700s—Thomas Chippendale, George Hepplewhite, and Thomas Sheraton.

Chinaware also came into its own in the 1700s with the work of Josiah Wedgwood and Josiah Spode. Wedgwood is best known for his blue jasperware with classical decorations in white. Three Josiah Spodes made pottery; father, son, and grandson. Their pottery was quite different from Wedgwood's. These two kinds of china still are important English exports.

Sometimes, of course, English people don't feel like going out. They can sit at home in front of the telly (television) and watch one of England's two major television networks, the BBC (British Broadcasting Corporation) or the IBA (Independent Broadcasting Authority). The BBC has no commercials. Television owners pay a yearly tax that helps support it. The IBA broadcasts commercials every half hour, but the programs themselves are not sponsored by the advertisers. Much of England's fine programming, such as "Masterpiece Theatre" and "Monty Python's Flying Circus," has found its way to other countries.

The royal wedding of Prince Charles and Lady Diana Spencer took place in 1981.

THOSE SPECIAL TIMES

England has many traditional days for celebration. Often they are based on functions of the government. In June there is "Trooping the Colour," when the queen reviews her troops. Then there is the State Opening of Parliament, when she rides through the streets in her horse-drawn state carriage. On that day, special guards from the Tower of London (called yeomen of the guard, or beefeaters) search the cellars of the Houses of Parliament to make sure kegs of gunpowder haven't been hidden there. This is because of the Gunpowder Plot that happened back in 1605.

On November 5 of that year, a man named Guy Fawkes and his cohorts tried to blow up King James I and the Houses of Parliament. The plot didn't succeed. But every year now on November 5, children make stuffed dummies called "guys." They go around begging "a penny for the guy" and collecting as much money as they can. Then they have a huge bonfire, burn the guys, and set off fireworks.

Other holidays, such as Christmas and Easter, also are surrounded with traditions and festivities in England. And when the coronation of a new king or queen or a royal wedding occurs, the whole country celebrates.

Trooping the Colour

Chapter 8

THIS EARTH OF MAJESTY

KINGS AND QUEENS—PLUS

Since the days of the Angles and the Saxons, England has been a land of kings and queens. Some, such as George I and George II, did very little of historical importance. Others, such as William the Conqueror, Henry VIII, and Elizabeth I, played extremely important parts in shaping England's—and the world's—history.

But not everyone who made tremendous contributions to England—and the world—sat on the throne. Some sailed the seas, some served on battlefields, some worked in basements or laboratories, and some sat at desks.

BRITANNIA, RULE THE WAVES

Francis Drake was not the first—or the last—Englishman to make his home on a ship. Drake was born about 1540. He grew up on an abandoned ship near the river Medway with his parents and eleven brothers. He decided to go to sea for a living and started as an apprentice on a merchant ship. By the time he was in his twenties, he owned the ship and was a captain.

Then the Spanish made the mistake of firing on his ship. Drake rushed back to England. He asked Queen Elizabeth I for a commission as a privateer. (A privateer was like a pirate with a license.) Soon Drake, in his flagship, the *Golden Hind,* was chasing the Spanish all over. He sank their ships and made off with their gold. Once, to avoid a counterattack, he got back to England by sailing completely around the world. Queen Elizabeth made him a knight for being the first Englishman to do this.

By this time England and Spain were at war. Slowly the great Spanish fleet, the Armada, prepared to attack her much weaker enemy. But Drake had a plan. He sailed down to Spain. He sank ships and exploded storehouses on the shore. It took the Spanish a while to recover. At last they sailed to Land's End on the southwestern coast of England. Drake and his commander Lord Howard of Effingham, were waiting for them. Several battles later, when the smoke had cleared, the Armada was destroyed. The Spanish had not managed to sink a single English ship.

Henry Hudson's name was given to Hudson Bay, Hudson Strait, and the Hudson River in North America. He really wanted to find a northern sea passage to the East and all its riches. That he never did, but he managed to have some unusual adventures.

Hudson set off in his ship, the *Hopewell,* to sail across the North Pole in 1607. He couldn't get through the ice and had to turn back. A second try also failed.

Then Hudson began working for a Dutch company. On the ship the *Half Moon* he sailed to what is now New York and up the river to the site of present-day Albany.

In 1610, Hudson set off on his last mission, again looking for that northern passage. On the ship *Discovery* he sailed through Hudson Strait and into Hudson Bay. Then the weather became a problem. Soon *Discovery* was frozen in. The men were able to get to land, but there wasn't much to eat when they got there.

Around 1900 Robert Scott used this ship on an Antarctic expedition.
It is permanently docked in the river Thames.

They were sick, hungry, and angry. At last, after one more attempt to sail on, they were frozen in again at Camp Digges. Here most of the sailors mutinied. They put Hudson, his son, and their sick comrades in a small boat, cut it loose, and sailed away. Neither the little boat nor the men's bodies ever were found.

James Cook was only thirteen years old in 1741 when he ran away to sea. He hadn't chosen an easy life. He was a cabin boy on an old coal boat. But Cook loved the sea and couldn't wait to learn all about it. By 1755 he was ready to join the navy.

Some years later he was sent to the South Seas with a group of scientists to make observations of the planet Venus. Once again he sailed on a coal boat. But this one, the *Endeavour*, was well fitted out for her voyage. After they had finished the astronomical observations, Cook had orders to search for new lands for the English crown. He discovered Australia and the two main islands of New Zealand. He also found a way to prevent his sailors from getting the disease known as scurvy by feeding them a proper diet. This not only saved many of their lives, but the lives of countless other sailors in the future.

On Cook's second important trip, he was asked to seek out a continent around the South Pole. Many people had guessed it was there. They felt sure it would be a good place to live. After dodging icebergs and sailing completely around Antarctica, Cook proved that no one would want to live there.

His third trip took him in search of Henry Hudson's famous northern passage. Cook proved once and for all that sailing across the top of North America was impossible. He also managed to discover the Hawaiian Islands on the way. He came back to them on his return voyage to England and, after a series of unfortunate happenings, was killed there by natives.

IN TIMES OF TROUBLE

In 1854, England, France, and Turkey were at war with Russia in the Crimea. At Scutari, on the shore of the Bosporus, there sat an English hospital for the treatment of soldiers wounded in battle. There weren't enough doctors and there was no material for making bandages. There were no nurses either. Rats and mice roamed the wards. Fresh laundry was almost unheard of and the old sewers stank.

To that place of pain and horror came Florence Nightingale, an English society girl. She had studied nursing in France and Germany, against the wishes of her family. Nursing was not considered a "nice" thing for women to do in those days. Florence Nightingale didn't care. All she cared about was her patients, the sick and wounded soldiers. As soon as she arrived at Scutari she started organizing and cleaning up. She trained other women as nurses and wrote letters to important officials back home who might be able to help.

Soon Florence Nightingale became known as "the soldier's angel" and "the lady with a lamp." At night she often moved through the wards with her lamp. She soothed those in pain and comforted the dying.

After two years the war ended. Florence Nightingale went back home. Her health was broken and she was to be an invalid for the rest of her life. But that didn't stop her. Her grateful country wanted to do something for her. She told them to start a school of nursing. In 1859 it opened at St. Thomas' Hospital. In 1861 the first class of thirteen nurses was graduated. Florence Nightingale had supervised much of the work from her own bed. She went on supervising others about nursing for the rest of her ninety years.

Florence Nightingale

One of the young women Florence Nightingale inspired was Edith Cavell, an Englishwoman born in 1865. For a number of years Nurse Cavell worked in the slums of London. Then she was invited to Belgium, a country that knew little about scientific nursing. She set up a school in a Brussels suburb and started teaching. Before long she had a staff of fifty nurses and was director of several hospitals.

Then in 1914, World War I broke out. At first it was all parades and brave young men marching off to war. When the wounded began arriving, the war showed its true colors. Many of Nurse Cavell's students had to leave. Some returned to their own countries and some nursed the wounded on the battlefields.

Early in the war, Belgium was occupied by the Germans. After a while, strange rumors began circulating in Nurse Cavell's clinic. Nurse Cavell was caring for British, French, and Belgian soldiers and then helping them to escape! That was dangerous business. But Edith Cavell was not afraid of danger. She helped more than two hundred soldiers to escape before the Germans arrested her and brought her to trial.

"I am a nurse. It is my duty to save lives," she told them. The Germans found her guilty and sentenced her to be shot.

A BETTER MOUSETRAP

The great ambition of all inventors is to be able to come up with a better mousetrap that will win fame and fortune for them. English mice don't seem to be in more danger than mice elsewhere in the world, but English inventors — and other scientists — certainly have been leaders in their field.

One of the first English scientists was Roger Bacon, a monk who was born in 1214. People didn't know much about science. Some of Bacon's ideas seemed strange indeed. He talked about the way convex lenses could magnify and about the power in gunpowder. He talked about the possibility of building — such nonsense! — a flying machine, an automobile, and a locomotive. Any man who talked like that should be censored, thought the people around him. For long periods of time Bacon was.

During the reign of Elizabeth I and in the 1600s, a new generation of scientists was born. William Gilbert wrote a book about magnetism. Robert Boyle discovered a law of chemistry (called Boyle's Law). He introduced many scientific methods to chemistry. Sir Isaac Newton first stated the law of gravitation. Edmund Halley discovered Halley's comet. Sir John Harrington invented the first flush toilet. (The queen immediately had one installed.) In the field of medicine, William Harvey discovered how blood circulates through the body.

In the 1700s, inventors came into their own. Flying shuttles, spinning jennies, spinning mules, power looms, and screw-cutting lathes paved the way for the Industrial Revolution. In 1774 Joseph Priestley discovered oxygen. This changed the whole approach to chemistry.

The nineteenth century brought the invention of the electric telegraph and modern cement. The discovery of a dye called "mauvine" by W.H. Perkins gave birth to the dye industry. D.E. Hughes sent out the first radio signals in 1878. And at the end of the century, in 1897, Sir Joseph Thomson discovered the electron.

But it was a quiet man, who liked to stay at home in Kent with his flowers and children around him, who dropped one of the biggest scientific bombshells ever to explode in England or anywhere else in the world. His name was Charles Darwin. Together with a colleague, Alfred Russel Wallace, he presented a series of scientific observations that they felt proved the existence of evolution. (Evolution is the theory that living things do not stay the same. They change over the years and centuries so they can survive better in the places they live.) All over the world Darwin's theory set people to noisy argument. For some, the question still is not settled.

Left: Shakespeare's home in Stratford-on-Avon
Below: The Royal Shakespeare Theatre

THE MIGHTY PEN

Back in the times of invading tribes and blazing campfires, some people in England traveled around and told stories. Eventually some of them started writing down their stories. From that simple beginning has sprung one of the richest treasures in the world. Miles of books have been written about English literature. Some scholars spend whole lifetimes studying one or another tiny area of it.

Geoffrey Chaucer (1340-1400) wrote his stories in verse, as did most people back then. His greatest work is *The Canterbury Tales*, written during the last fifteen years of his life. In it, different tales are told by a group of people making a religious pilgrimage to Canterbury. Some of the tales are funny, some are adventurous, some are clever. Taken together, they tell us about the age in which Chaucer lived—and about people who live in any age.

About 150 years after Chaucer died, Queen Elizabeth I came to the throne. England enjoyed a period of literature as star-spangled as any in world history. Although Edmund Spenser (1552-1599) worked as a clerk, his heart was that of a poet's. From his pen came the wonderful fantasy *The Faerie Queene*.

Christopher Marlowe (1564-1593) was a man who told the truth as he saw it. He got in a great deal of trouble as a result. Marlowe was stabbed to death in a tavern brawl when he was only twenty-nine years old. But he left behind some great plays, including *The Tragical History of Doctor Faustus*.

The brightest star in English literature—and maybe in any literature—is William Shakespeare (1564-1616). He didn't spend much time in school. But he knew how to use his eyes and ears— and his mind and pen. When he was eighteen years old, he wed a woman named Anne Hathaway. The marriage didn't work out. Eventually Shakespeare left Anne behind in Stratford-on-Avon and went to seek his fortune in London.

There he met a group of actors and began his career, acting in plays, but above all, writing them. *Romeo and Juliet, Macbeth, A Midsummer Night's Dream, Hamlet, The Tempest, Othello,* and *King Lear* are just a few of his plays. Many were performed at a theater in London called the Globe. The crowds loved them.

John Milton (1608-1674) began writing poems while he was still in school. His greatest poem, though, came much later in his life. He was blind when he wrote his masterpiece, *Paradise Lost.* It is a very long poem (called an epic), based on the book of Genesis in the Bible.

Alexander Pope (1688-1744) was a small, hunchbacked man whose health always gave him trouble. Besides that, he was a Roman Catholic at a time when England was not fond of Catholics. But Pope could write. He vented his anger and pain in brilliant poems called satires. Two of his most famous poems are *The Rape of the Lock* and *An Essay on Man.* Pope's works were filled with little nuggets of wisdom. "Fools rush in where angels fear to tread." "A little knowledge is a dangerous thing." "To err is human, to forgive divine." Pope said all of them—first.

William Wordsworth (1770-1850) lived a quiet life, mostly in the Lake District in northern England. He cared about nature and its rewards. Some of his best-known poems are "Lines Composed a Few Miles Above Tintern Abbey," "I Wandered Lonely as a Cloud," and "Ode on the Intimations of Immortality."

Samuel Taylor Coleridge (1772-1834) was a friend of Wordsworth. He spent time with him in the Lake District. Coleridge was a restless man with a brilliant imagination.

Poet William Wordsworth is buried in Grasmere village churchyard in the Lake District National Park.

Lord Byron is buried in Poet's Corner in Westminster Abbey. Some other important writers buried here are Alfred Tennyson, Edmund Spenser, and Ben Jonson.

Unfortunately he was addicted to opium. Two of his finest poems are "The Rime of the Ancient Mariner" and "Kubla Khan."

By this time the novel had been born in England. One of the greatest novelists was Jane Austen (1775-1817). She was the daughter of a country clergyman and lived a quiet life. But her eyes, her ears, and her mind were busy—watching, listening, and thinking about what went on with people. She put these people—or people like them—into her novels. Her work mixes a strong dose of common sense with a sense of humor. Some of her novels are *Pride and Prejudice, Mansfield Park,* and *Emma.*

Lord Byron (1788-1824) was a handsome, moody, adventurous man—the perfect romantic hero. Many of the poems he wrote, such as *Don Juan* and *Manfred,* were about people like himself. Byron cared passionately for freedom. He traveled to Greece to help revolutionaries overthrow their Turkish rulers. He caught a fever there and died when he was only thirty-six years old.

Charles Dickens (left) is remembered for works such as Oliver Twist *and "A Christmas Carol." One of his less famous works is* The Old Curiosity Shop *featuring the shop (right) that can be visited today in London.*

Percy Bysshe Shelley (1792-1822) was another romantic hero who died young. Shelley was what is known as a nonconformist. He didn't agree with established ideas and he didn't want anyone to tell him what to do. He wrote some beautiful poems, such as "Ode to the West Wind" and "To a Skylark." Shelley drowned when a storm overturned his small boat in Italy.

John Keats (1795-1821) loved and searched for beauty. Although he began to study medicine, his spare time was spent writing poems. But just about the time he seemed to be succeeding in life, Keats found that he was dying of tuberculosis. Some of his greatest poems are "The Eve of St. Agnes," "Ode on a Grecian Urn," and "Ode to a Nightingale."

Charles Dickens (1812-1870) was born a poor boy. He had to work in a gloomy warehouse before he was ten years old. When he grew up, he began writing for newspapers. But he never forgot what it was like to be poor. Many of his novels were written to show just how bad life was for some people. Some of his most famous works are the novels *Oliver Twist* and *David Copperfield.*

Charlotte Brontë (1816-1855) and her sister Emily Brontë (1818-1848) lived in a small manufacturing town on the edge of a Yorkshire moor. Their life was very difficult. But both of them were determined to write and they did. Charlotte's novel, *Jane Eyre,* and Emily's, *Wuthering Heights,* are two of the best-loved books of all time.

The story of Elizabeth Barrett Browning (1806-1861) and Robert Browning (1812-1889) is somewhat like a fairy tale. Elizabeth Barrett hurt her back when she was fifteen. From then on she had to stay at home. Elizabeth wrote poems. One day Robert Browning, who also was a poet, read one of them and wrote to her. They exchanged letters and poems for about a year. Then one day Robert carried Elizabeth away from her father's house. He wed her and took her off to Italy where they lived together happily until her death sixteen years later. Some of Robert's most famous poems are "Pippa Passes," "My Last Duchess," and "The Pied Piper of Hamelin." Elizabeth is best known for her collection of love poems, *Sonnets from the Portuguese.*

Some of the stars of English literature have written especially for children. Lewis Carroll wrote *Alice's Adventures in Wonderland* and *Through the Looking-Glass.* Beatrix Potter both wrote and illustrated such delightful little stories about animals as "The Tale of Peter Rabbit," "The Tale of Mrs. Tiggy-Winkle," and "The Tale of Pigling Bland." C.S. Lewis's *The Chronicles of Narnia* tells of the adventures of children in a world of fantasy. J.R.R. Tolkien created another fantasy world in *The Lord of the Rings.*

Chapter 9

THIS LITTLE WORLD

Small but rich—that's England. The English people realize this. They try to take care of what they have, whether it's an oil well on the ocean floor, the air in a city, or a single rose in a garden. They've made some mistakes in the past, just as people have in other parts of the world. For a while it seemed as if factories would trample nature underfoot. But—just in time—the English took a good look at what really mattered. Now it seems that the natural treasures on this island will remain for generations of English people—and tourists—to come.

The English also work hard to preserve their historical treasures. Places such as Stonehenge, Runnymede, and Stratford-on-Avon are important to people all over the world who care about history, justice, and art. English people want to be sure that these places—and many others—will be there for visitors who come to look and remember.

England's role in world affairs has changed since the two World Wars. She is no longer head of a great empire. Her future is uncertain. But one thing *is* certain. England has given uncountable treasures to the world in the areas of law and government, science, and the arts and literature. No doubt she will go on contributing—perhaps in some surprising ways—in the future.

Visitors to the city of Bath are impressed by the Roman Bath and Bath Abbey (opposite). In Herefordshire they are charmed by the thatched-roof houses (above).

England has done many things. She has made and exported many things to the rest of the world. But her greatest national product has always remained the same—her people. Some have been kings or queens or prime ministers. Some have been writers or scientists or scholars. Some have kept shops or swept streets or raised families. Together they have given their country the courage and creativity needed to make her great in good times and bad. Together they have made "this little world" of England an "earth of majesty."

Cities and towns in England   Lowercase letters refer to map insert on bottom left

Place	Ref	Place	Ref	Place	Ref
Aldershot	E6	Friern Barnet	k12	Oxford	E6
Alnwick	C6	Gainsborough	D6	Penzance	E4
Aylesbury	E6	Gateshead	C6	Peterborough	D6
Banbury	D6	Gillingham	E7	Plymouth	E4
Barking	k13	Gloucester	E5	Poole	E5
Barnstaple	E4	Grantham	D6	Portsmouth	E6
Barrow-in Furness	C5	Gravesend	E7, m13	Preston	D5
Basingstoke	E6	Greenwich (part of London)	m13	Ramsgate	E7
Bath	E5	Grimsby	D6	Reading	E6
Bedford	D6	Guildford	E6, m11	Reigate	E6, m12
Bedlington	C6	Harlow	k13	Ripon	C6
Berwick-upon-Tweed	C6	Harrogate	C6	Rochdale	D5
Beverley	D6	Hartlepool	C6	Rugby	D6
Bexhill-on-Sea	E7	Harwich	E7	Ryde	E6
Bideford	E4	Hastings	E7	St. Albans	E6, k12
Birkenhead	D5	Hemel Hempstead	k12	Salisbury	E6
Birmingham	D6	Hereford	D5	Scarborough	C6
Bishop's Stortford	E7	Hertford	E6, k12	Scunthorpe	D6
Blackburn	D5	High Wycombe	E6	Sevenoaks	m13
Blackpool	D5	Hoddesdon	k13	Sheffield	D6
Blyth	C6	Hull	D6	Sheringham	D7
Bodmin	E4	Hythe	E7	Shrewsbury	D5
Bolton	D5	Ilford	k13	Sidmouth	E5
Boston	D6	Ilfracombe	E4	Skegness	D7
Bournemouth	E6	Ipswich	D7	Slough	k11
Bradford	D6	Isle of Wight	E6	Smethwick (Warley)	D5
Bridgwater	E5	Keighley	D6	Southampton	E6
Bridlington	C6	Kendal	C5	Southend-on-Sea	E7
Brighton	E6	Kettering	D6	Southport	D5
Bristol	E5	Kidderminster	D5	South Shields	C6
Bude	E4	King's Lynn	D7	Spalding	D6
Burnley	D5	Lancaster	C5	Stafford	D5
Burton-on-Trent	D6	Launceston	E4	Staines	m11
Cambridge	D7	Leamington	D6	Stockport	D5
Canterbury	E7	Leatherhead	m12	Stoke-on-Trent	D5
Carlisle	C5	Leeds	D6	Stratford-on-Avon	D6
Chelmsford	E7	Leicester	D6	Sunderland	C6
Cheltenham	E5	Lewes	E7	Sutton-in-Ashfield	D6
Chesham	k11	Leyton	k12	Swindon	E6
Cheshunt	k12	Lincoln	D6	Taunton	E5
Chester	D5	Liverpool	D5	Tiverton	E5
Chesterfield	D6	London	E6, k12	Torquay (Torbay)	E5
Chichester	E6	Loughborough	D6	Trowbridge	E5
Chigwell	k13	Louth	D7	Truro	E4
Chingford	k13	Lowestoft	D7	Tunbridge Wells	E7
Cirencester	E6	Ludlow	D5	Tynemouth	C6
Colchester	E7	Luton	E6	Ulverston	C5
Coventry	D6	Macclesfield	D5	Wallasey	D5
Cowes	E6	Maidstone	E7	Wallington	m12
Crewe	D5	Malton	C6	Wallsend	C6
Darlington	C6	Manchester	D5	Walsall	D6
Dartmouth	E5	Mansfield	D6	Warrington	D5
Derby	D6	Margate	E7	Warwick	D6
Doncaster	D6	Maryport	C5	Wembley	k11
Dorchester	E5	Middlesbrough (Teesside)	C6	West Bromwich	D6
Dorking	m12	Minehead	E5	Weston-Super-Mare	E5
Dover	E7	Newark	D6	Weymouth	E5
Dudley	D5	Newbury	E6	Whitby	C6
Durham	C6	Newcastle-on-Tyne	C6	Whitehaven	C5
Eastbourne	E7	New Malden	m11	Winchester	E6
Edmonton	k12	Newport	E6	Wisbech	D7
Ely	D7	Newquay	E4	Wolverhampton	D5
Epping	k13	Northampton	D6	Woodford	k13
Epsom	m12	North Walsham	D7	Wood Green	k12
Esher	m12	Norwich	D7	Woolwich	m13
Exeter	E5	Nottingham	D6	Worcester	D5
Exmouth	E5	Okehampton	E4	Workington	C5
Eyemouth	C5	Oldham	D5	Worthing	E6
Falmouth	E4	Orpington	m13	Yeovil	E5
Folkestone	E7	Oswestry	D5	York	D6

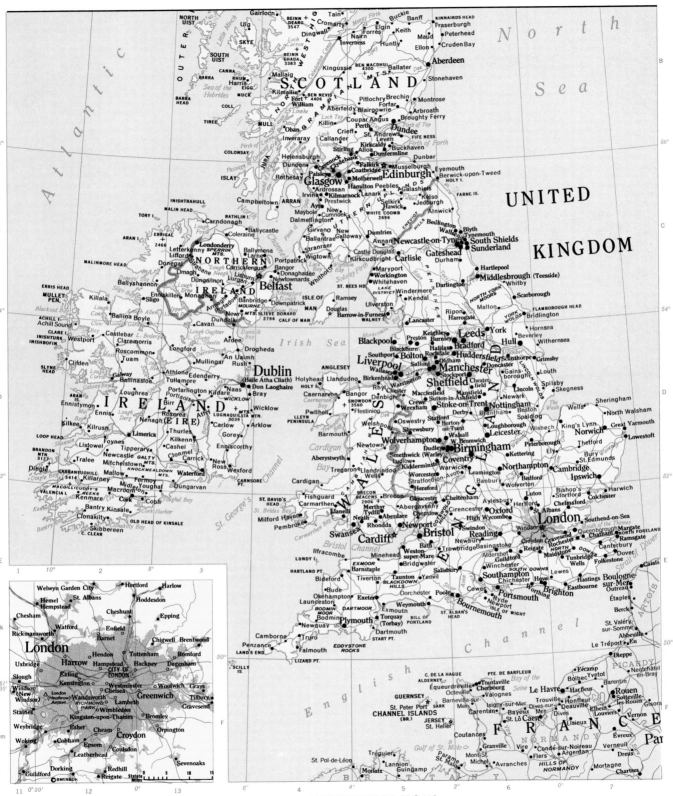

© Copyright by RAND McNALLY & COMPANY, R. L. 82-S-113

Statute Miles

Conic Projection

MINI-FACTS AT A GLANCE

GENERAL INFORMATION

Official Name: England

Capital: London

Official Language: English

Government: England is part of the United Kingdom of Great Britain and Northern Ireland, which also includes Northern Ireland, Wales, and Scotland. England is a constitutional monarchy. The king or queen is head of state but does not rule the country. The country is governed by a prime minister and cabinet ministers. Parliament consists of the House of Lords and the House of Commons. An election is held every five years. All citizens over the age of eighteen may vote in national elections. The country is divided into administrative counties that consist of urban and rural districts.

Flag: The United Kingdom flies the Union Jack, a red, white, and blue flag with a large red cross. This is more popular than England's unofficial flag, called St. George's Cross.

Coat of Arms: England uses Great Britain's coat of arms, which features three lions and a unicorn.

National Song: "God Save the Queen"

Religion: The Church of England is the official state church, but England has religious freedom. More than 27 million people belong to the Church of England. There are more than 4 million Roman Catholics and about 450,000 Jews. Other religious groups are Muslims, Hindus, Sikhs, and Buddhists.

Money: Pounds and pence. One hundred pence equals one pound. One pound equaled approximately $1.60 (United States currency) in 1982. Paper bills are issued in denominations of 1, 5, 10, 20, and 50 pounds. Coins are 1/2, 1, 2, 5, 10, and 50 pence and 1 pound.

Weights and Measures: England uses the metric system. Weight is often given in stones. One stone equals 14 pounds.

Population: 46,821,000 (1986 estimate) Seventy-nine percent of the people live in cities. England has one of the highest population densities in the world.

Cities: There are six major urban areas called conurbations. The largest cities in these areas are:

London	7,028,200
Birmingham	1,004,030
Liverpool	574,560
Manchester	530,580
Leeds	500,200
Bradford	292,340
Wolverhampton	269,530
Newcastle-on-Tyne	212,430

(Population figures based on 1976 census.)

GEOGRAPHY

Highest Point: Scafell Pike, 3,210 ft. (978 m)

Lowest Point: The Fens near Ely, sea level

Rivers:
Thames . . . . 215 mi. (346 km)
Severn . . . . 210 mi. (338 km)
Trent . . . . 170 mi. (274 km)

Lakes: Most of England's large lakes are in the Lake District. The largest lake is Windermere, 10.5 mi. (17 km) long and 1 mi. (1.6 km) wide.

Mountains: England's main mountain range is the Pennine Chain. Many of England's "mountains" are really only low hills.

Climate: It is never very cold or very warm in England. A very hot day in summer is only 80° F. (26.7° C.). It seldom snows in England. The average temperature in winter is 40° F. (4.4.° C.). The average temperature in summer is 60° F. (15.6° C.). It is very rainy. The average rainfall in England is 34 in. (86 cm).

Greatest Distances: North to south, about 360 mi. (579 km)
East to west, about 270 mi. (435 km)

Area: 50,362 sq. mi. (130,438 km2)

NATURE

Trees: The most common trees in England are the oak, elm, ash, and beech.

Birds: There are 230 different kinds of birds in England.

Insects: There are 21,000 varieties of insects.

Snakes: There are only three species of snakes. One, the adder, is poisonous.

Animals: Small mammals include the fox, hare, hedgehog, rabbit, weasel, shrew, rat, and mouse. There are fewer kinds of animals in England than in the rest of Europe.

EVERYDAY LIFE

Food: Typical Sunday dinner is roast beef or lamb (called a joint), vegetable, potato, and pie with hot custard sauce. A common snack is fish and french fries (called chips). Most people drink tea at most meals, but a great deal of coffee also is drunk.

Homes: Most English families live in small houses. A typical family house has three small bedrooms, a living room, kitchen, and garage. Many houses are attached to neighboring houses. About one third of all houses do not have central heating.

Holidays:

New Year's Day, January 1
Good Friday
Easter Monday
Early May Bank Holiday (first Monday in May)
Spring Bank Holiday (last Monday in May)
Summer Bank Holiday (last Monday in August)
Christmas Day
Boxing Day, December 26

Culture: London has more than five hundred libraries. The largest is in the British Museum. There are 450 museums and art galleries in England. Most cities or large towns have museums of natural history and art galleries. The largest museum is the British Museum. There are many theaters in England, especially in an area of London called the West End.

Recreation: People love gardening and grow flowers in small gardens or in flower boxes. Flower shows are popular. Families usually spend vacations at the seaside in a place such as Brighton. Television is popular but it isn't free. Everyone who owns a television set must pay for a license each year.

Sports: England's most popular sport is football (soccer). The football season runs from August to May. Most towns have cricket teams. Rugby is played from late summer to spring. There are 2,600 lawn bowling clubs. Other popular sports are golf, horse racing, polo, sailing, tennis, swimming, rowing, hunting, fishing, and fox hunts.

Communication: There are 4,400 newspapers and magazines published in England. The government owns the post office and telephone and telegraph services. About 11 billion letters are sent each year.

Transportation: In London people use taxis, bicycles, cars, buses, and the subway (called the underground) to get to work. Around the country people travel by train, airplane, or car. England has about 2,000 mi. (3,218 km) of navigable inland waterways.

Schools: There are about 37,000 schools, 44 universities, and The Open University, which teaches courses by radio, television and mail. All children must attend school between the ages of five and sixteen years. Ninety percent of the children attend government schools and ten percent attend private schools. Many children attend preschools. In England private schools are called public schools. Famous universities are Oxford University, Cambridge University, and the University of London.

Principal Products:
Agriculture: Cattle, dairy products, sheep, fruit, barley, potatoes, wheat.
Fishing: Sole, herring, haddock.
Manufacturing: Iron and steel, chemicals, airplanes, automobiles, machinery, pottery and porcelain, woolen and cotton cloth and yarn, silverware.
Mining: Coal, iron ore.

IMPORTANT DATES

8000-3000 B.C. — First settlers in England arrive from Spain and Brittany (France)

2000 B.C. — Beaker Folk arrive

700 B.C. — Celts arrive

55-54 B.C. — Julius Caesar invades Britannia

A.D. 43 — Roman armies conquer Britain and set up colonies

400s — Romans return home

800s — Danes invade England

1066 — Battle of Hastings won by William the Conqueror

1215 — King John signs the Magna Carta

1282 — England and Wales united

1295 — Model Parliament called by Edward III

1314 — Scotland wins Battle of Bannockburn and becomes independent

1337-1453 — England and France fight the Hundred Years War

1455-1485 — The War of the Roses fought by two royal families

1513 — Henry VIII invades France

1514 — England and France sign a peace treaty

1517 — Martin Luther posts Ninety-five Theses which lead to the Reformation

1534 — King declared head of Church of England

1536 — Sir Thomas More tried and executed for treason

1536 — Henry VIII unites Wales and England

1540 — Thomas Cromwell arrested and executed for treason

1603—England and Scotland united by accession of James I to the throne

1605—Guy Fawkes arrested for Gunpowder Plot

1620—Pilgrims leave Plymouth, England, aboard the *Mayflower*

1642—Civil war between monarchy and Parliament

1649—England becomes a commonwealth

1660—Monarchy restored by Parliament

1665—The Great Plague

1666—The Great Fire of London

1679—Habeas Corpus Act is passed

1688—Glorious Revolution ends

1689—Bill of Rights passed

1694—Bank of England founded

1702—First daily newspaper published

1707—England, Scotland, and Wales united as the United Kingdom of Great Britain

1765—Stamp Act passed

1776—American colonies issue their Declaration of Independence from England

1805—Battle of Trafalgar fought and control of the seas returned to Great Britain

1806—Napoleon issues the Berlin Decree proclaiming blockade against the British Isles

1807—Slave trade ended by Parliament

1812—The War of 1812

1815—Battle of Waterloo fought

1828—London University founded

1833—The Factory Act makes it illegal for children under nine to work in factories

1834 — A fire destroys the Houses of Parliament

1891 — A second act makes it illegal for children under eleven to work in factories

1914 — Britain declares war against Germany

1922 — The British Broadcasting Company is formed

1926 — A national strike of many workers declared

1936 — First regular television service begins in the London area

1939 — Britain declares war against Germany

1948 — National health program begins

1956 — World's first nuclear power plant opens in Calder Hall

1970 — A second national strike declared

1979 — Margaret Thatcher becomes the first woman prime minister

1982 — Falkland Island crisis, Argentina and England at war. Argentina surrenders June 14

FAMOUS PEOPLE

Jane Austen (1775-1817), writer, born in Steventon, Hampshire

Roger Bacon (1214-1294), scientist and philosopher, born in Ilchester, Somerset

Thomas à Becket (1118-1170), church leader, born in London

Robert Boyle (1627-1691), scientist, born in Lismore, County Cavan

Charlotte Brontë (1818-1848), writer, born in Thornton, Yorkshire

Elizabeth Barrett Browning (1801-1861), poet, married to Robert Browning, born in Durnham

Robert Browning (1812-1889), poet, married to Elizabeth Barrett, born in London

George Gordon Byron (1788-1824), poet, born in London

Lewis Carroll (1832-1898), pen name of Charles Lutwidge Dodgson, writer, born in Daresbury, Cheshire

Edith Cavell (1865-1915), nurse, born in Swardeston, Norfork

Geoffrey Chaucer (1340-1400), poet, born in London

Thomas Chippendale (1718-1779), furniture maker, born in Otley, Yorkshire

Winston Churchill (1874-1965), prime minister, born in Blenheim Palace, Oxfordshire

Samuel Taylor Coleridge (1772-1834), poet, born in Ottery St. Mary, Devonshire

James Cook (1728-1779), mariner and explorer

Oliver Cromwell (1599-1658), Lord Protector of England, born in Huntingdon, Huntingdonshire

Charles Darwin (1809-1882), naturalist, born in Shrewsbury

Charles Dickens (1812-1870), writer, born in Portsmouth

Benjamin Disraeli (1804-1881), prime minister, born in London

Francis Drake (1540-1596), explorer, born in Devonshire

Guy Fawkes (1570-1606), plotted Gunpowder Plot to blow up the Houses of Parliament, born in York

William Gilbert (1540-1603), scientist, born in Colchester, Essex

William S. Gilbert (1836-1911), playwright, born in London

William E. Gladstone (1809-1898), prime minister, born in Liverpool

Edmund Halley (1656-1742), astronomer, born in London

William Harvey (1578-1657), scientist, born in Folkestone

Rowland Hill (1772-1842), soldier, born in Press Hall, Shropshire

Henry Hudson (?-1611), navigator, birthplace unknown

D. E. Hughes (1831-1900), inventor, born in London

Inigo Jones (1573-1652), architect, born in London

John Keats (1795-1821), poet, born in London

David Lloyd George (1863-1945), statesman, born in Manchester

Christopher Marlowe (1564-1593), playwright, born in Canterbury

John Milton (1608-1674), poet, born in London

Horatio Nelson (1758-1805), naval hero, born in Burnham Thorpe, Norfolk

Isaac Newton (1642-1727), scientist, born in Woolsthorpe

Florence Nightingale (1820-1910), nurse and hospital reformer, born in Florence, Italy

Robert Peel (1788-1850), prime minister, born in Bury, Lancashire

Alexander Pope (1688-1744), poet, born in London

Joseph Priestley (1733-1804), scientist, born in Fieldhead

Walter Raleigh (1552-1618), navigator, born in Hayes Barton, Devon

William Shakespeare (1564-1616), playwright and poet, born in Stratford-on-Avon

Percy Bysshe Shelley (1792-1822), poet, born in Warmham

Edmund Spenser (1552-1599), poet, born in London

Arthur Sullivan (1842-1900), composer, born in London

J. R. R. Tolkien (1892-1973), writer, born in South Africa

Wat Tyler, started a revolt against taxes, killed by Lord Mayor Walworth on June 15, 1381

Alfred Russel Wallace (1823-1913), naturalist, born in Monmouthshire

Robert Walpole (1676-1745), prime minister, born in Houghton Hall, Norfolk

William Wordsworth (1770-1850), poet, born in Cockermouth

Christopher Wren (1632-1723), architect, born in East Knoyle, Wittshire

RULERS OF ENGLAND

Saxons	Reign
Egbert	802-839
Ethelwulf	839-858
Ethelbald	858-860
Ethelbert	860-866
Ethelred I	866-871
Alfred the Great	871-899
Edward the Elder	899-924
Athelstan	924-939
Edmund I	939-946
Edred	946-955
Edwy	955-959
Edgar	959-975
Edward the Martyr	975-978
Ethelred II	978-1016
Edmund II	1016

Danes	
Canute	1016-1035
Harold I	1035-1040
Hardecanute	1040-1042

Saxons	
Edward the Confessor	1042-1066
Harold II	1066

Normans	
William I, the Conqueror	1066-1087
William II	1087-1100
Henry I	1100-1135
Stephen	1135-1154

Plantagenet Family	
Henry II	1154-1189
Richard I	1189-1199
John	1199-1216
Henry III	1216-1272
Edward I	1272-1307
Edward II	1307-1327
Edward III	1327-1377
Richard II	1377-1399

House of Lancaster	
Henry IV	1399-1413
Henry V	1413-1422
Henry VI	1422-1461

House of York	
Edward IV	1461-1470

House of Lancaster	
Henry VI	1470-1471

House of York	
Edward IV	1471-1483
Edward V	1483
Richard III	1483-1485

House of Tudor	
Henry VII	1485-1509
Henry VIII	1509-1547
Edward VI	1547-1553
Lady Jane Grey	1553
Mary I	1553-1558
Elizabeth I	1558-1603

House of Stuart	
James I	1603-1625
Charles I	1625-1649

Commonwealth	
Long Parliament	1649-1653

Protectorate	
Oliver Cromwell	1653-1658
Richard Cromwell	1658-1659

House of Stuart	
Charles II	1660-1685
James II	1685-1688
William III	1689-1702
and Mary II	1689-1694
Anne	1702-1714

RULERS OF GREAT BRITAIN

House of Hanover

George I	1714-1727
George II	1727-1760
George III	1760-1820
George IV	1820-1830
William IV	1830-1837
Victoria	1837-1901

House of Saxe-Coburg-Gotha

Edward VII	1901-1910
George V	1910-1917

House of Windsor

George V	1917-1936
Edward VIII	1936
George VI	1936-1952
Elizabeth II	1952-

PRIME MINISTERS

Name	Party	Dates Served
Robert Walpole	Whig	1721-42
Lord Wilmington	Whig	1742-44
Henry Pelham	Whig	1744-54
Duke of Newcastle	Whig	1754-56
Duke of Devonshire	Whig	1756-57
Duke of Newcastle	Whig	1757-61
Duke of Newcastle	Whig	1761-62
Lord Bute	Tory	1762-63
George Grenville	Whig	1763-65
Lord Rockingham	Whig	1765-66
William Pitt	Whig	1766-68
Duke of Grafton	Whig	1768-70
Lord North	Tory	1770-82
Lord Rockingham	Whig	1782
Lord Shelburne	Whig	1782-83
Duke of Portland	Tory	1783
William Pitt (The Younger)	Tory	1783-1801
Henry Addington	Tory	1801-04
William Pitt (The Younger)	Tory	1804-06
Lord Grenville	Whig	1806-07
Duke of Portland	Tory	1807-09
Spencer Perceval	Tory	1809-12
Lord Liverpool	Tory	1812-27
George Canning	Tory	1827
Lord Goderich	Tory	1827-28

Name	Party	Dates Served
Duke of Wellington	Tory	1828-30
Earl Grey	Whig	1830-34
Lord Melbourne	Whig	1834
Sir Robert Peel	Tory	1834-35
Lord Melbourne	Whig	1835-41
Sir Robert Peel	Tory	1841-46
Lord John Russell	Whig	1846-52
Lord Derby	Conservative	1852
Lord Aberdeen	Tory	1852-55
Lord Palmerston	Liberal	1855-58
Lord Derby	Conservative	1858-59
Lord Palmerston	Liberal	1859-65
Lord John Russell	Whig	1865-66
Lord Derby	Conservative	1866-68
Benjamin Disraeli	Conservative	1868
William E. Gladstone	Liberal	1868-74
Benjamin Disraeli	Conservative	1874-80
William E. Gladstone	Liberal	1880-85
Lord Salisbury	Conservative	1886
William E. Gladstone	Liberal	1886
Lord Salisbury	Conservative	1886-92
William E. Gladstone	Liberal	1892-94
Lord Rosebery	Liberal	1894-95
Lord Salisbury	Conservative	1895-1902
Arthur Balfour	Conservative	1902-05
Sir Henry Campbell-Bannerman	Liberal	1905-08
Herbert H. Asquith	Liberal	1908-16
David Lloyd George	Liberal	1916-22
Andrew Bonar Law	Conservative	1922-23
Stanley Baldwin	Conservative	1923-24
James Ramsey MacDonald	Labor	1924
Stanley Baldwin	Conservative	1924-29
James Ramsey MacDonald	Labor	1929-35
Stanley Baldwin	Conservative	1935-37
Neville Chamberlain	Tory	1937-40
Winston Churchill	Conservative	1940-45
Clement Attlee	Labor	1945-51
Sir Winston Churchill	Conservative	1951-55
Sir Anthony Eden	Conservative	1955-57
Harold Macmillan	Conservative	1957-63
Sir Alec Douglas-Home	Conservative	1963-64
Harold Wilson	Labor	1964-70
Edward Heath	Conservative	1970-74
Harold Wilson	Labor	1974-76
James Callaghan	Labor	1976-79
Margaret Thatcher	Conservative	1979-

A country house built of stone in northeastern England

INDEX

Page numbers that appear in boldface type indicate illustrations

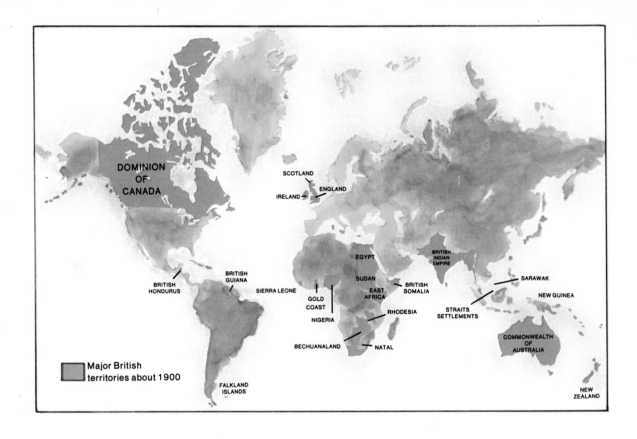

DOMINION
OF
CANADA

SCOTLAND

ENGLAND

IRELAND

EGYPT

BRITISH
INDIAN
EMPIRE

SARAWAK

BRITISH
GUIANA

SUDAN

BRITISH
HONDURUS

SIERRA LEONE

GOLD
COAST

EAST
AFRICA

BRITISH
SOMALIA

NEW GUINEA

NIGERIA

RHODESIA

STRAITS
SETTLEMENTS

COMMONWEALTH
OF
AUSTRALIA

BECHUANALAND

NATAL

Major British
territories about 1900

FALKLAND
ISLANDS

NEW
ZEALAND

About the Author

Carol Greene has a B.A. in English Literature from Park College, Parkville, Missouri and an M.A. in Musicology from Indiana University, Bloomington. She's worked with international exchange programs, taught music and writing, and edited children's books. She now works as a free-lance writer in St. Louis, Missouri and has had published over 20 books for children and a few for adults. When she isn't writing, Ms. Greene likes to read, travel, sing, and do volunteer work at her church. Her other books for Childrens Press include: *The Super Snoops and the Missing Sleepers; Sandra Day O'Connor: First Woman on the Supreme Court; Rain! Rain!; Please, Wind?; Snow Joe;* and *The New True Book of Holidays Around the World.*